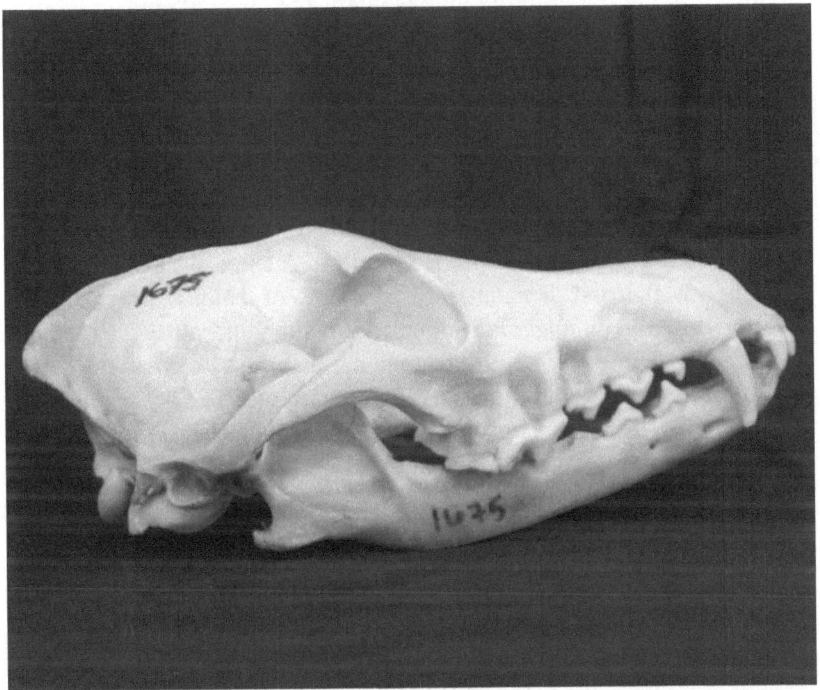

Americans Hate Coyotes

How the War on America's Song Dog Began and Why it
Persists: A Collection of Essays

Preface

My goal behind the publication of this book is to shed light on the hypocrisy in wildlife management in the United States. In my opinion, the management of *Canis latrans* throughout the United States has been largely driven by ancient, Old West mentality and partiality toward hunting and agricultural communities.

There is an interesting interplay between human psychology, management ethics, and animal cognition when it comes to the coyote. In this debate, conspiracy theories, fierce anthropomorphism, and politicization of science are all rampant. Distrust of scientists is one area of major concern regarding the management of carnivores in general, as Americans tend to be quite trigger-happy when it comes to North American wildlife. Scientific research is the only credible method by which it can (and has) been proven that lethal management of coyotes does not work.

Excessive reliance on lethal control for coyotes is costly, ineffective over long periods and has tremendous off-target effects. The Federal Agency, Wildlife Services, is on record for having killed thousands of state- and federally-protected species over the years, as a direct consequence of indiscriminate lethal measures intended for coyotes.

The state our world is in right now no longer lends itself to polite conversation. L, for one, am tired of scientists having to be diplomats and take the abuse, ruthless slandering, baseless criticism and systematically-encouraged distrust of legitimate scientific research. We need to face the facts and can out the ethical neglect and partiality of our wildlife managers.

Here are the facts.

Americans Hate Coyotes

Foreword: The Erasure of Coyote First Person

A tale as old as time: European settlers come into a country in which they've never once set foot, claim it as their own, and – as they've never lived or persisted in said country – their complete misunderstanding and lack of regard for the newly-stolen land begins to wreak havoc on the ecological dynamics of the native environment.

There has always been something that bothers me about the way people – not just of European descent, but all North Americans – talk about coyotes, and native predators in general: as if they are something to be removed, a pest of sorts, an inconvenience.

This is something that has almost never made sense to me – these animals have been here for *millions of years* before us, and yet, somehow, we have the audacity to believe that this environment would be better off without them, and with humans as the sole apex instead? Coyote derbies, organized nation-wide slaughter of the species by local, state, and federal governmental authorities, and even the language with which this species is discussed (both colloquially and in the media), are all reflective of the erasure of what the coyote truly is in an ecological and cultural sense.

When we ask ourselves how such blatant, severe mismanagement of a native species – especially an apex predator integral to the health and persistence of ecological dynamics throughout the continent – has continued for so long, we cannot afford to overlook the ties wildlife management has to environmental racism and the erasure of marginalized communities – in this case, Indigenous peoples.

When we empower authorities with the ability to take the lives of wildlife with no prior scientific or ecological training, what benefit does that offer? When whole communities refuse to learn how their actions effect the wildlife that is being forced to share space with us as a direct result of increasing rates of urbanization and encroachment on natural habitat, what does that say about our values as a society? When we neglect to learn the significance of a species not only on its natural physical environment, but its meaning to entire cultures and, apart from that, its intrinsic value, can we really say we are managing and researching wildlife for the love of non-human animals?

No, instead wildlife management – especially in consideration of the obsession with the reduction of "wildlife damage" with the use of lethal measures rather than behavioral changes in human society – our focus has instead turned to the accessibility of convenience and comfort for humanity as a direct result of separation from nature.

As we continue to face the dangerous effects of our rapidly-deteriorating world, we must begin to call bias for what it is and take accountability for our actions, especially in the ways they directly affect the natural world.

One thing that has been particularly difficult to articulate is the way I am drawn to, and identify with, the coyote in terms of marginalization and erasure of culture. What does this mean, you ask?

The coyote has long been a figure of both good and bad in Indigenous cultures, and, regardless of the way the animal is depicted in the stories that are passed down through the generations, it is a species that rests at the core of the belief systems of these communities and their relationships to the natural world. The villainization of the coyote is directly in line with the dehumanization of Indigenous peoples and the devaluation of their cultures and beliefs.

Americans Hate Coyotes

The Coyote is not – and has never been – just the "coyote." This species is a representation of the beginnings of Indigenous peoples and places, and in some belief systems, is even an active participant in decolonization – a symbol of hope and tenacity in the face of Indigenous erasure. The coyote;s name is not "alone," but *Italpas, Ma'ii, Mica, Skinkuts, Tcu-unnkita,* and *Isil.* It is not just a trickster, but a savior, a child of the moon, genderless or masculine or feminine, a child, or a leader. Above all, an ancestor.

> *Settler colonialism relies on the continued erasure and silencing of Indigenous epistemologies and knowledges to prevent challenges to settler colonial claims to land and history, and to subvert Indigenous efforts of decolonization. Settler colonialism is reaffirmed continuously through western languages, ideologies, policies, institutions and philosophies as articulated through a western epistemological framework of education, law and government that does not engage with decolonization, and actively resists the unsettling of these ideologies.* –
> Cutcha Risling Baldy, *Decolonization: Inidigeneity Education & Society*

Baldy, C. R. (2015). Coyote is not a metaphor: On decolonizing, (re)claiming and (re)naming Coyote. *Decolonization: Indigineity, Education & Society*, 4(1), 1-20.

The continued erasure of the significance of the coyote to Indigenous cultures and the ecology of North American ecosystems is a powerful contributor to the continued lethal force used against this species.

As an African American woman, I feel for the coyote when I ponder the hatred North Americans have for this species based on the offense of it simply... existing. Civilians have been documented calling for the lethal removal of coyotes that have been observed simply standing in a suburban street. Although many have expressed in surveys that the coyote is surely valuable to the health of North American ecosystems, those same individuals in the same questionnaires expressed that they do not wish for the to exist in any proximity to their own residence[27]. *The coyote should be allowed to exist, yes, but just not near me* is the sentiment.
This is certainly a valid sentiment to hold, don't get me wrong. However, when this stance is then translated into violence because of the discomfort individuals have based on a lack of understanding and/or compassion, or disregard for the animal's life, it becomes a different issue entirely.
The existence of this animal is not as fluffy and cuddly as that of our domestic dogs, and because that is something many people do not want to realize, they would rather do away with it completely and suppress scientific research that opposes the comfort of Old Western ideology than take accountability for anthropogenic activity on native North American wildlife.
In order to make real, effective progress in wildlife management and human interaction with the natural world, we must first step away from the erasure of scientific research and Indigenous (the two are not separate) knowledge, free ourselves from the confines of European colonialist mentality and begin to value and respect native wildlife intrinsically.
The perpetuation of the coyote's portrayal as a pest has largely come from the hunting and agricultural community – yes, urbanites have had their fair share of negative interactions with this species, but American cultural disdain for the species does not originate in suburbia. Speaking informally, many

hunters view the coyote as a competitor of sorts, consuming the deer they have been stalking on their trail cameras or otherwise beating them to the prey. Ranchers hold a deeply-rooted abhorrence for the species, as the coyote is responsible for many a loss of livestock, sometimes adding up to a significant loss of income that can severely financially cripple rural families.

Still, this does not excuse the negligence of wildlife managers to adhere to current scientific literature and place greater effort in reducing indiscriminate lethal practices that have – year after year – resulted in significant losses of not only native North American wildlife, but species that are protected by federal law. Wildlife authorities have access to said literature, whereas, often, agricultural and hunting professionals/hobbyists do not, rendering their ideologies to be largely based on loose generational folklore, cultural bias, and anecdotal evidence.

The beginning of change is the acquisition of knowledge. This book is my contribution to that change. May we use this information well.

Contents

This book is dedicated to my Uncle Lloyd. I love you always.

Chapter 1. The Inception of the War Against Coyotes

Between 1865-1890, when 3 million European families were settling the Western United States, prey species such as bison (*Bison bison*), mule deer (*Odocoileus hemonius*), elk (*Cervus elaphus*) and pronghorn (*Antilocapra americana*) were driven to dangerously low numbers – the bison nearly going extinct – and ultimately replaced with domesticated livestock. Because carnivores retained their "[pre-settlement] abundance"[9], wolves (*Canis lupus*) and coyotes (*Canis latrans*) specifically, depended on the abandoned carcasses. Yet, as the decline in prey species populations began to take effect, these predators turned their attention to livestock, beginning the "campaign of large-scale predator extermination"[9].

Interest for state and private bounties for extermination began to wane in 1900, and livestock owners lobbied for federal involvement in predator removal. In response, the United States Department of Agriculture (USDA) Forest Service collaborated with the Bureau of Biological Services (BBS) and received the necessary congressional funding in 1915. By 1939, livestock owners and the federal government teamed up to create and fund the Division of Predator Animal and Rodent Control (PARC) under BBS, which was succeeded by the US Department of the Interior's (DOI) Animal Damage Control (ADC), to ultimately become what is now, Wildlife Services (WS). This agency operates under USDA Animal Plant and Health Inspection Services (APHIS), and to this day, WS still operates primarily under the 1931 ADC Act (7 U.S.C. §426), which allows funding by private stakeholders, so opening up the space for conflicts of interest[9].

WS has operated this way for over a century, and, despite numerous name changes and department transfers, somehow still resists legislative change despite criticism from scientific committees and interest groups such as the American

Society of Mammalogists, scientific research which proves their lethal methods are dangerously indiscriminate, costly and inviable, and public opposition[1, 9, 24, 27, 53].

The origin of this agency is important, as it has been shown that communities which have a history of lethal control toward predators such as coyotes have deeply-set negative perspectives on the species which is the target of lethal control, and that these views are, more often than not, based on myth and word-of-mouth rather than legitimate scientific research or ecological fact. That said, I argue that, because of this history – not only of WS but the United States as a nation, due to the experience of early settlers, which were largely influenced by the culture of agricultural communities, *C. latrans* has been the victim of disproportionate lethal control by the federal agency, USDA APHIS WS, and state legislation such as that of California's Mammal Hunting laws (California Code of Regulations, CCR T14 §472-475) and California Fish and Game Code (CA FGC) Division 4 Chapter 3 Articles 1 and 2. I argue that the prejudice against this species is due to severe, negative anthropomorphism, neglect of legitimate, credible scientific research, and the vested interests of agricultural communities and politicians. The resulting intense pressure on this species worsens the very problem it aims to eliminate: human-coyote conflict.

The Mission Statement of WS is as follows:

"The mission of the Animal and Plant Health Inspection Services, Wildlife Services (WS), is to provide Federal leadership in managing conflicts with wildlife. WS recognizes that wildlife is an important public resource greatly valued by the American people. By its very nature, however, wildlife is a highly dynamic and mobile resource that can cause damage to agriculture and property, pose risks to human health and safety, and affect natural resources. WS conducts programs of research, technical assistance, and applied management to resolve problems that occur when human activity and wildlife conflict with one another"[90].

Immediately, there are biases introduced in the mission and core purpose of this agency. Even without knowing its history, one can see that its priorities are highly anthropocentric, having little regard for the ecological functions and reality of the wildlife it claims to respect. Here, it is framed that wildlife can "affect" natural resources: in a later directive, the WS *Mission and Philosophy*, the agency goes on to say that wildlife "… causes significant damage to agricultural crops and livestock, forests, pastures, property and infrastructure in urban and rural areas, and threatened and endangered species and their habitats"[90]. Right away, the question arises: How does a native species "damage" the forest that it naturally lives in, or the prey species that it, by trophic obligation, consumes? The only way that this can be justified is if the priority is human use and consumption of these natural resources. When the natural behaviors of a predator species such as *C. latrans* are framed this way, it then becomes justifiable to describe natural behavior as "damage:" as it presents an inconvenience to human recreational or commercial use of resources.

Coyote Ecology, Cognition and Related Management

Wildlife damage management is defined by USDA APHIS WS as "the alleviation of damage or other problems caused by or related to the presence of wildlife"[90]. This is quite a vague definition and, according to WS annual data reports from 1996 to 2018, wildlife damage encompasses all things from depredation on livestock to an unwanted animal simply being present at a golf course.

WS Directive: *Integrated Wildlife Damage Management Program* (IWDM) claims to take an integrative approach to the alleviation of wildlife damage. What this should mean is that actions include more than just lethal control, and that management efforts are quite evenly balanced between these actions. Take Alaska's invasive species management, for example (although *C. latrans* is not an invasive species, there are many parts of the US in which it is a non-native species, introduced primarily through the extirpation of the gray wolf, *C. lupus*, in a large part of its historical range): Alaska's management efforts of the invasive European rabbit (*Oryctolagus cuniculus*) included eradication, monitoring of the European rabbit and affected species such as the European green crab (*Carcinus maenas*), intervention (eradication, control, prevention, containment and population monitoring), research – which accounted for about one-quarter of expenditures – and education and outreach[78].

Compared to the state of Alaska's approach to the management of this species, WS spending is quite frivolous and heavily biased toward lethal control. In fact, between 1996 and 2018, hardly any coyotes were listed in the "Dispersed/Relocated" category and were overwhelmingly listed in the "Killed/Euthanized" category. This has resulted in the eradication of hundreds of thousands of coyotes annually before 2005 when it decreased to 70,000-80,000 annually and the practice of destroying den sites began to be recorded. Bergstrom *et al.* (2013) suggested that despite these devastating numbers, these reports may still be underestimated, as it has been said that the agency does not, in fact, report *all* the animals it has killed.

Coyotes are an extremely ecologically plastic species. Research has shown that they exist on a continuum, and that existence, and consequential ecological functioning, is directly influenced by its habitat: may it be rural, sub-urban, grassland, woodland, etc. Further, urban coyote populations tend to be more bold and exploratory than parapatric populations[12; 26; 23; 31; 62; 76; 77]. From this research, it can be inferred that not all of these subpopulations share the same prey species, or even have access to the same prey species. Because of this, these subpopulations have varying ecological functions:

Parapatric: habitats that are directly adjacent to one another, but not overlapping a coyote in a coniferous forest would feed on rodents, lagomorphs, mustelids, and cervids as carrion, another in an urban city would feed on anthropogenic food waste and small pets, and a rural coyote would feed on rodents which occur in the pastures, and, of course, small livestock such as calves, goats and sheep. Additionally, in each of these ecosystems, there are different life histories in coyote ecology: some occur as transient individuals, and others live in a resident pack, where only the alpha male and female reproduce[36, 76].

Ellington & Gehrt (2019) demonstrated that coyotes display a mix of synanthropic (positive response to urbanization in the form of increased population density in urban spaces *versus* natural environments, habituation to human activity and presence) and misanthropic (negative response to urbanization manifested in the alteration of movement and behavior, spatially and temporally, to avoid human presence and activity) behaviors to urbanization: In highly urbanized spaces, coyotes maintained much larger, yet highly fragmented territories. These territories were, on average, twice as large as those in natural spaces, and three times larger than suburban territories, and significantly more fragmented than both[26]. Across all habitat types, coyotes spent similar amounts of time avoiding humans, but more time traveling between patches in highly urbanized landscapes[26]. Finally, in highly urbanized landscapes, coyotes were more likely to display greater variation in behavior and movement between individuals, leading to the conclusion that urban coyotes are more inclined to exhibit behavioral syndromes, making each and every individual unique in the way it responds to control and exclusion measures [8; 52].

Barret *et al.* (2019) described five aspects that can contribute to a species' ability to learn and response to human presence, thereby overcoming challenges to colonize human-dominated spaces: innovation (the development of new, or modification of current behaviors in order to solve problems); behavioral flexibility (capability of altering behaviors in responses to environmental change, or inhibition of behaviors that were successful before, but are no longer); neophilia (inclination to be attracted to novelty); boldness (an individual's willingness to engage in risky behavior); and categorization (or generalization, an ability to assign specific responses to novel stimuli by avoidance or cessation of certain behaviors based on particular cues of the stimuli). The interaction of these factors in *C. latrans* has allowed it and other nuisance species to evade control measures such as *reactive* behavioral modification practices, exclosures, and baited traps. These management methods, especially when employed inconsistently, provide further novel stimuli and an opportunity for learning, rather than producing the desired dishabituation[8].

Given all of these dynamics in coyote ecology, especially in consideration of the emergence and persistence of unique behavioral syndromes within populations[8, 12, 76], and continuously rising levels of habituation in urban populations especially[26], it makes little sense to employ a single management technique as if they were all one. Research has shown that the species can become virtually a completely different animal in its behavioral and movement patterns and ecological roles depending on its habitat of choice: natural, rural, suburban or urban. Despite this growing wealth of knowledge on *C. latrans*, WS and associated agencies continues to rely on lethal control as the sole means of curbing human-wildlife conflict, and they do so indiscriminately (Table 1.1).

Year	(Federal) Organization	(Federal) Total Killed/Euthanized	(State) Participating States	(State) Reported Harvest
1996	WS	79655	42	226613
1997	WS	82390	42	275406
1998	WS	77997	38	215691
1999	WS	85938	40	244365
2000	WS	85955	39	252546
2001	WS	88868	35	194535
2002	WS	173719	36	213140
2003	WS	75724	36	283377
2004	WS	75674	34	271018
2005	WS	72817	Total	2176691
2006	WS	87850		
2007	WS	90326		
2008	WS	89252		
2009	WS	81711		
2010	WS	80657		
2011	WS	83242		
2012	WS	76120		
2013	WS	75326		
2014	WS	61704		
2015	WS	68905		
2016	WS	76963		
2017	WS	69041		
2018	WS	68292		
2019	WS	62002		
2020	WS	62701		
2021	WS	64131		
2022	WS	56089		
Total		2154049		

Table 1.1 *Total of coyotes reported as killed to USDA APHIS Wildlife Services by year at the hands of various state agencies and Wildlife Services directly.*[98-120] *This table's data was compiled also using publicly available USDA APHIS WS program data reports 10T, 11, and G throughout 1996-2022.*

Lethal management is also dangerous for the ecological balance of all of the aforementioned ecosystems, as research has shown that a number of "rebound effects" can occur, including dynamic alterations in ecosystem functioning, behavioral changes in *C. latrans*, and increased populations[46, 53]. Once an individual from, or a whole breeding pair is removed lethally or permanently by other means, space opens up for the occupancy for another individual. These individuals are typically transients, which are – more often than resident coyotes – associated with problematic behaviors[11 43]. Transient individuals have been found to display more bold and exploratory behavior lending them to engage in riskier, more conflict-inducing behaviors. As Schell *et al.* (2018) found, parents are capable of passing such behaviors on to offspring, especially behaviors associated with habituation. As adults are removed and replaced with transient individuals, this increases the potential of creating litters of coyotes that are increasingly inclined to bold and exploratory – overall conflict-inducing behaviors – with every generation.

This is why statutes such as California's Mammal Hunting laws, CCR T14 §472-475 and CA FGC Division 4 Chapter 3 Articles 1 and 2 are so dangerous. State and federal authorities claim to base management practices on the best, most recent, credible research, however, it is demonstrated here that the most recent research has shown that, ecologically, lethal control is, in fact, one of the more dangerous avenues to take in coyote management. It was only in 2014 that the state of California banned the infamous coyote hunting derbies: where hunters gather and compete for monetary or other rewards as a prize for killing the most, or biggest, coyotes. This said, it is important to reiterate that the numbers recorded over the years represent only the total of coyotes taken by WS, and do not include those killed by hunters, private landowners, and local authorities given legal permission to kill coyotes upon request of affected citizens within their jurisdiction.

Draheim (2012) showed that American communities have already begun to abuse this system, and the history of wildlife management and socioeconomic standing in such communities are a direct influence on how they respond to the presence of coyotes in their neighborhoods. Draheim (2012) assert that human-wildlife conflict is "an outward manifestation of other social issues and basic beliefs about wildlife...[and] perception of conflict can be as, if not more, important than actual physical conflict between people and wildlife"[24].

It was found that residents of more affluent neighborhoods, or more urbanized areas, tend to hold stronger negative views than those who either currently live in, or have some sort of experience in, rural areas. This means that they are more prone to biased perspectives on coyotes and coyote management, and – more importantly – are more likely to misrepresent or exaggerate reports to authorities about coyote sightings and incidents, and less likely to be willing to accept their presence in human-dominated landscapes. For instance, at the foundational level, the cities of Greenwood Village, CO (more affluent in terms of education, income, and overall socioeconomic status) and Centennial, CO (less affluent) legally defined the term "incident" as it relates to coyotes, quite differently: (a) Greenwood Village, *incident*: "an unsafe situation where a coyote displayed abnormal behavior"[24]; (b) Centennial, CO, *incident*: "a conflict between a human and a coyote where a coyote exhibits behavior creating an unsafe situation for the human"[24]. Centennial citizens and authorities clearly have a more objective view, not only of coyotes but of urban wildlife management.

Draheim (2012) also discussed the fact that the town of Greenwood Village gave legal authority to the local police – who were provided with no prior wildlife management or ecology education or training – sole authority to lethally remove coyotes on sight after citizen complaints. Their research showed that the residents of Greenwood Village were significantly more likely than Centennial residents to call authorities for occurrences including hearing coyotes howling at night, seeing coyotes near playing children, seeing a coyote on their property and more[24]. None of these behaviors are indicative of aggression or potential danger, but instead, are indicative of fear-mongering and misinformation provided to the public regarding coyote behavior.

Further, although research into the behavioral and movement ecology of *C. latrans* in suburban to highly urbanized landscapes is sparse, it has been shown that coyotes show high amounts of individual variation in all aspects of behavior and movement in these ecosystems[26]. From this it can be inferred that coyotes display unusually high levels of behavioral syndromes within the species, in addition to parapatric variation in ecological functions and niches and life histories (resident vs. transient)[5; 8; 12; 26; 30; 39; 62; 76; 77].

Public Perspectives on Management and Coexistence

As previously mentioned, WS operations are widely opposed by both professional institutions and organizations and the general public. For decades now, there have been calls for transformative change in not only the legislation on which WS practices and authority are based, but on the actions and purpose of WS itself.

Drahem *et al.* (2019) assert that human-wildlife conflict is "an outward manifestation of other social issues and basic beliefs about wildlife"[24] and that perception that conflict can – and should – be considered as equally important as the physical manifestations of conflict between humans and wildlife. Returning to the examples of Greenwood Village, CO, and Centennial, CO, communities' relationships with wildlife and the natural world as a whole are influenced by two types of relationships: relationship with political authority and with historical belonging.

Sarkki *et al.* recalled the Environmental Cuznets Curve Theory, which holds that, in "post-industrial," or "developed," societies, concern for the environment and consequential protection of that environment increase linearly with economic development. However, Sarkki *et al.* (2019) note that the opposite has been observed in western society, namely, the United States. Aspects that have influenced this are the lack of social innovation (SI) as a consequence of strained relationships and distrust between the public and political authorities, specifically, the federal government. Relational values, on which these relationships are based are as follows: i. *Doing*: an individual's perspective on nature's contributions to themselves and the community, whereby the value of those contributions is manifested in opportunities offered by nature, ii. *Belonging*: a "communal dimension" of values, expressed as the experience and feeling of " 'being at home' in social collectives"[74], and iii. *Respecting*: environmental and social justices that can be recorded and analyzed temporally, for example, by institutional changes (i.e. federal legislative change) and cultural changes in favor of environmentalism[74]. All of these relational values operate on both the individual and collective scale, and so are interconnected. However, where one is compromised, so are the others.

In the United States, the strains between the general public and federal/state/local governments are tangible. In the case of lethal control of apex predators such as *C. latrans*, those strains are stressed even further. In this case, we have a compromise of *Respect*, where federal authorities do not respect the values of *all* affected constituents (not only those stakeholders and citizens who consumptively use natural resources, such as hunters and agricultural professionals, but non-consumptive users such as hikers and wildlife photographers) and rather prioritize a small subset of the nation's population. Where the upholding of this relational value fails, there is damage inflicted upon the others, and therefore the entire structure. Where one does not feel respected, there is no true communal role, no sense of true belonging, instead, the feeling and reality of being ostracized due to opposing values. This leads to a lack of *Doing*, where now the majority of the general public either find themselves indifferent, and therefore inactive on such atrocities as the disproportionate lethal measures taken against *C. latrans*, or, such as in the case of Greenwood Village, falling into historical tradition of erroneously believing lethal control is the only way, despite ample evidence against this notion.

Sarkki *et al.* (2019) found that when measures were implemented to deliberately involve the public in management plans and practices, not only did relationships between citizens and the government improve but, because the entire system worked more smoothly and efficiently, the health and overall well-being of the environment and affected wildlife increased in quality.

There are many ways in which these findings can be implemented. One way, which is discussed very widely, is the implementation of community "hazing," whereby behaviors such as making noise, throwing small objects and waving one's arms around startles a coyote (or any unwanted nuisance species) into avoiding humans and human-dominated landscapes, ultimately leading to the desired dishabituated behavior. Reports on results of the implementation of hazing have been mixed due to two main issues: use of hazing is extremely community-dependent – it cannot depend on only one person, and if even one person breaks ranks (by feeding and other such attractant behaviors) the system falls apart. Secondly, managers and communities too often find themselves using hazing as a *re*active technique when it is most effective *pro*actively.

Much *et al.* (2018), by studying non-lethal management methods on *C. lupus*, found that animals who were already conditioned to novelty items and circumstances were 11 times faster to engage in investigative behaviors than unconditioned individuals, and four times faster to engage in work (attempts to solve novel challenge) behaviors. This bold and exploratory behavior is reinforced by food rewards, which for an animal in a human-dominated landscape can mean a plethora of things from anthropogenic resources. Individuals who earned these food rewards by engaging in investigative and work behaviors were significantly more likely to engage in these behaviors again in the future. Much *et al.* assert that, although it is difficult to implement nonlethal measures, and that dishabituation is not necessarily synonymous with unlearning behaviors, nonlethal measures are most valuable as preventative measures and can "mediate a carnivore's ability to explore and shape their experience"[52] with anthropogenic resources by decreasing, and ultimately removing, learning opportunities and therefore possibilities of conflict-inducing behaviors[52].

An important component of the effectiveness of nonlethal management is human behavior. Elliot *et al.* (2016) found evidence that "people will not... make the connection between coyote behavior, human behavior, and resulting conflict"[27] and, at times, will continue to engage in risky or attractant behaviors despite past negative experiences, or refuse to engage in behaviors to encourage coyote dishabituation (i.e., hazing). For example, 74% of respondents reported that they had lost a pet to a coyote, yet 42% of respondents still engaged in the most common coyote-attractant behavior: leaving pets outside unattended[27]. Additionally, they found that people whose attitudes towards coyotes were generally positive refused to "harass" the animals by engaging in hazing behaviors, a choice that ultimately leads to more human-coyote conflict[27]. Attractant and risky behaviors noted by Elliot *et al.* included intentional feeding (feral cats [*Felis catus*] or coyotes themselves), unattended pet food, and bird feeders are all primary drivers in coyote habituation as these factors attract the animals into human-dominated landscapes, and further reinforce this bold behavior with food rewards[27, 74].

Conclusively, it can be said that human-coyote conflict is not simply driven by the ecological plasticity of *C. latrans*, but largely by human behavior as well. Yet, the coyote is still negatively anthropomorphized, or villainized, as a species that is dangerous and needs to be done away with.

Chapter 2. The Fallacy of Lethal Control

As humans continue to encroach on wild habitat, the issue of invasive and pest species becomes increasingly prevalent all throughout the world. One of the most widespread, and rapidly dispersing, invasive species – which began as a native species – known here in the United States, is the coyote, Canis latrans. In 2011, the USDA estimated that, in the preceding five years, coyotes accounted for 53.1% of an approximate loss of USD 98.5 million in cattle alone[76]. C. latrans is also a known host of diseases including Lyme disease, rabies, plague, tularemia, mange, and distemper[16, 21, 79, 122].

The ongoing division on the management of *C. latrans* is focused on two main management alternatives: lethal and nonlethal control. Lethal control takes a variety of forms, ranging from the removal of "problem individuals,"[11; 46], to eradication of local sink populations, to government authorized culling activities, namely from Wildlife Services, an agency of United States Department of Agriculture[9]. Nonlethal control focuses mainly on the behavioral modification and exclusion of habituated individuals[7, 11, 53], changes in human behaviors that attract coyotes to urban and suburban areas[27] and translocation[43]. In this review, I will discuss why nonlethal management is the more sustainable – in terms of cost-efficiency, social welfare and ecological benefits, which in turn, influence economic losses and gains on both local and national scales.

As public opinion toward wildlife continues to shift positively toward a more conservation-centered, non-use value and away from an anthropocentric perspective[9, 43, 90], the management alternative of lethal control is not only becoming less palatable, but it has also been repeatedly shown to be the least cost-effective control strategy of the two[9, 53, 78], with little to no ecological benefits, potentially bring more detriment than solution[9, 42].

It has been suggested that despite ample evidence that nonlethal management is the more effective and sustainable management alternative, the continuation of lethal management can be largely attributed to the desire of certain communities and individuals to continue to assimilate to historical cultural norms[9, 53, 64]. Other drivers of this perpetuation can be attributed to pluralistic values[45, 51, 64] including cultural norms[9, 53] a misinformed desire to be close to wildlife[27], or a potential biological control method of feral cat species[32], and free riding[45, 53, 64].

Cost-Benefit Analysis of Lethal versus Nonlethal Control

Research has shown that nonlethal management can save large amounts of money for managers, communities, and individuals[53] while lethal management can be costly and extremely inefficient[9, 78]. McManus *et al.* (2015) conducted a three-year study on 11 livestock farms in the Eastern Cape Province of South Africa, using lethal management for the first year, and nonlethal for the remaining two. Accounting for running lethal control costs in the first year, implementation and running costs for nonlethal control in the second, and running costs for nonlethal control in the third, McManus *et al.* (2015) found that converting to nonlethal control saved farmers USD 13.79 per head of livestock, with a mean stock of USD 1,501, which totaled to an average of USD 20,699 per farmer. The decline in depredation for the first year was 69.3% and 72.7% in the second year.

Nonlethal control methods varied throughout the farms, including livestock guardian dogs, alpacas, and "Dead-Stop" livestock protection collars. All farmers were trained on how to identify the cause of livestock death (depredation, disease, other), and when necessary, an external expert opinion was acquired.

Although the change in control methods was shown to provide significant savings, two farms ultimately reverted to lethal management post-study, five farms combined lethal and nonlethal management and four farms held to nonlethal practices. (It is important to note that, for 9 out of 11 farms, nonlethal control methods were sponsored for the duration of the study. The choice of continuation in either method was left to individual discretion, and the farmer took on the financial responsibility of his/her choice.)

McManus *et al.* (2015) go on to discuss that these choices, particularly those to revert to lethal control, were not "purely… economic decision[s]… driven more by cultural norms and satisfaction than economics." McManus *et al.* (2015) assert that "Hunting of carnivores is often culturally and socially embedded and may provide intangible benefits such as social prestige and enjoyment"[53].

This sentiment is echoed in the Bergstrom *et al.* (2014) article on the United States Department of Agriculture agency, Wildlife Services (WS). Bergstrom *et al.* (2014) recount the staggering numbers of wildlife species killed by the agency between the years 1990 and 2011. The animals killed were federally listed as Endangered (E) or Threatened (T), or were petitioned to be listed as either E or T during this time period, totaling to be 137,393 animals of 15 different small- and large-bodied mammalian species, carnivorous, omnivorous and herbivorous, but all considered to be "pests" or "invasive" to those calling for WS services. *C. latrans* was one of the top four target species. According to Bergstrom *et al.* (2014), "[S]ince 2000, WS has killed – intentionally and unintentionally – 2 million native mammals… numerous state-protected mammals, and 15 million native birds including – unintentionally – protected golden eagles (*Aquila chrysaetos*) and bald eagles (*Haliaeetus leucocephalus*)."

It is clear that WS holds a strong bias to service the hunting and ranching/agricultural population of the United States as their management practices target certain native game species over other, particularly, native carnivorous species of wildlife. The history of WS reflects this as well, as it began due to lobbying from livestock farmers desiring predator eradication, after "state and private bounties on predators became unreliable"[9]. Despite historic and continued criticisms from groups such as The American Society of Mammalogists, along with the general public, WS persists under legislation from the 1931 ADC Act[9].

The economic problems associated with WS activities occur primarily as a consequence of mesopredator release[9]. Bergstrom *et al.* employ several examples of this, including the fact that wolves the Greater Yellowstone Ecosystem naturally target old and diseased elk. In their absence, the potential for the spread of disease through local elk populations is greatly increased. This disease spread can then affect other native ungulate populations, and ultimately "decrease ecosystem resilience" and create vacancies for invasive species to then fill. Consequentially, this incurs costs not only for habitat restoration, due to changing dynamics of local flora species, unchecked in the reduced presence of herbivores, but also in invasive surveillance and control and costs of reintroducing gray wolves (which, since 1974, has cost USD 43 million)[9]. Bergstrom *et al.* (2014) refer to Cole (1970) on the fact that, in Arizona, there was an estimated 5:1 cost-benefit ratio for lethal control of coyotes in relation to livestock depredation, translating to another significant economic loss due to WS activities.

An additional example of invasive species management in Alaska, where it was estimated that, between 2007-2011, the total cost of invasive species management was USD 29 million, with the most spending dedicated to eradication of three species: Norway rats (*Rattus norvegicus*), northern pike (*Esox Lucius*) and European rabbits (*Oryctolagus cuniculus*). USD 5 million was dedicated to the eradication and follow-up monitoring of *R. norvegicus* alone[78].

Mesopredator: predator species that is not an apex predator, and is preyed upon by other predator species.

The Collective Action Problem

Keohane & Olmstead (2007) describe a "collective action problem" to be when "a collection of individuals – people, or firms, or even nation-states – may find itself in a situation where the group as a whole is better off if all contribute to the common good, but each individual member of the group has incentives to free ride." On a local scale, the prime example for the collective action problem on invasive species management, specifically related to the coyote, is the California law, enforced by California Fish and Game Commission (CFGC), which allows *C. latrans* to be hunted "at any time of year and in any number" with few restrictions on time of day and method of hunt.

This is despite ample evidence against the mass killing of [functionally] invasive species like coyotes, which induces a rebound effect, which the HSUS describes as a circumstance in which the reproducing alpha pair of coyotes are replaced by potentially problematic, transient individuals and more offspring are then produced, thereby worsening the original problem. To combat this problem, policies need to be changed to better regulate this form of consumptive use of natural resources.

While in the realm of governmental practices, to mention WS again, Bergstrom *et al.* (2014) claim that agriculture is the "primary beneficiary" of federal wildlife control, which is biased in favor of "western ranchers." They go on to discuss that the benefitting livestock producers free ride by "[externalizing] the costs of predator losses via government-subsidized predator control"[9]. This study showed that WS has conflicting interests in terms of wildlife management, and this is especially disconcerting with the realization that primary urban invasive species, including *C. latrans*, are among their main targets. According to current research, the lethal management WS employs endangers countless communities, leaving them vulnerable to either increased local populations of invasive species, increased chances of disease transmission or general discomfort due to invasive/pest presence, and significantly increased externality costs associated with habitat degradation, invasive species control and surveillance, native species reintroduction and more[9].

Finally, in McManus *et al.* (2014) and Pienaar *et al.* (2015), it was found that continuation of, or reversion to, lethal control practices was primarily a choice of free riders who did not take on the cost of management themselves (one farmer chose lethal management post-study, as it was managed by a neighbor)[53], individuals who desired to maintain cultural tradition[53, 64], lack incentive due to potential financial losses in business and/or lifestyle (minimum land stewardship to avoid increased lease payments, land conversion or sales)[64], or those motivated by a deep-set distrust for governmental authority/involvement[64].

To scientists, educated activists and individuals who are generally passionate about animal and environmental wellness, the case of lethal vs. nonlethal control of *C. latrans* seems to a clear one. However, there is a colossal amount of intersectionality in legal, social and economic concerns regarding this issue.

On an individual level, one may struggle with a general affection toward wildlife. This is shown in Elliot *et al.* (2016) where they found that individuals who had a positive attitude toward wildlife were more likely to engage in coyote attractant behaviors, furthering the problem of *C. latrans* presence in urban/suburban landscapes, and increasing habituation levels of the animal, ultimately making it more dangerous to humans. One could reasonably expect that this same individual, due to his/her positive attitude toward wildlife, would not support lethal removal of the animal. Additionally, Elliot *et al.* (2016) suggest that 51.% of respondents "enjoy wildlife in their neighborhood," as 49.4% of those surveyed agreed that "coyotes are an important part of nature in their county," yet the pluralism is highlighted by the fact that, in the same survey, 38.5% of respondents said that coyotes "should not be tolerated close to people."

This is a clear reflection of the pluralistic values that come along with coyote management. Even in the studies by McManus *et al.* (2015) and Pienaar *et al.* (2015), pluralism is made clear when the economic benefits of nonlethal management are made clear during the study, yet at the conclusion, participants revert to lethal control due to cultural values and convenience. This is not to say that they do not value these savings and the protection of their livestock, but as Mason (2006) suggests, these are differing bearers of value, where the values of cultural traditions and convenience are higher than those of long-term economic savings. These participants display akrasia (Mason [2006] refers to Nussbaum [1986] and Wiggins [1980] to define this as "weakness of will," and why an individual would choose a "worse" alternative) in the making of this choice between lethal and nonlethal management (Mason 2006).

Nonlethal management is clearly the better, more sustainable, most economically beneficial management alternative. It avoids the rebound effect,
which *effectively* reduces invasive species abundance, reduces negative effects of invasive species presence (in the context of *C. latrans*: primarily disease transmission, predation on pets, livestock economic losses, general human-coyote conflict) by behavioral modification of target species (and behavioral changes for humans engaging in attractant behaviors) and remains aligned with current public values in terms of wildlife and environmental welfare.

The economic savings (USD 20,699 per farmer) and increased mean profit:loss ratios for the farmers (2.11:1 in the first year of nonlethal control, 1.23:1 in the second year compared to the first) in the McManus *et al.* (2015) study are undeniable.

I believe that the natural follow-through with these results would be to move into a partial community-based management plan. Pienaar *et al.* (2015) discussed distrust for governmental agencies preventing members of the public from choosing the economically efficient alternative. This issue can, over time, be cured by employing methods such as those in

McManus *et al.* (2015) where farmers were trained in livestock loss identification. Elliot *et al.* (2016) suggest that agencies/managers target animal/nature lovers over the general public, as, not only are they the primary demographic engaging in attractant behaviors, but they are also the most likely to participate in community-based management, nonlethal alternatives. Education on basic coyote ecology, avoidance of attractant behaviors such as leaving food/produce or small pets outside, training on community-level hazing and the development of a standardized reporting system for sighting and incidents[11, 27], would be a strong start for community involvement in nonlethal management practices.

Studies by Baker (2016) and Holden *et al.* (2016) provide the most cost-effective methods by which managers should employ surveillance efforts. Their findings can be applied in the context of coyote management to say that constant sampling (no varying levels of effort over time) is most beneficial.

Chapter 3. The Cunning Canid

Relatively little is known about the cognitive ethology of *Canis latrans*, the coyote. The domestic dog, *C. lupus familiaris*, has become a popular model organism in the past 20 years for the study of the evolutionary development of cognitive ecology and social learning. These studies have been largely comparative in nature, however, they have almost exclusively focused on the cognitive abilities of *C. l. familiaris* as it relates to *C. lupus lupus*. I have yet to see an application of this knowledge to any other species in Canidae.

Studies that have focused on the behavior and cognitive abilities of *C. latrans* are shockingly rare. I believe that this is in part due to the persecution this species faces, being seen almost exclusively as a nuisance species, and consequentially having studies focused primarily on control and eradication methods and effects rather than ethological value and uniqueness. With the expansion of human populations into natural spaces all over the world, and increased interactions between humans and wildlife, particularly carnivores, knowledge of the cognitive skill and ethological adaptivity of Carnivora species is going to have significant implications for wildlife management and reduction of human-wildlife conflicts.

The United States currently leans heavily on lethal management of *C. latrans*, as it is the leading species of livestock depredation, accounting for 53.1% of depredation losses of calves and 40.5% of cattle depredation losses in 2015 (where total depredation by coyotes, cougars, bobcats, dogs, vultures, wolves, bears, and other/unknown predators accounted for 5.2% of all livestock deaths nationwide)[85]. Regarding sheep, coyotes accounted for 54.3% and 63.7% of adult and lamb losses in 2015, respectively, where the total deaths due to depredation nationwide in the same year were 1.8% of adults and 3.9% of lambs (USDA *et al.*, 2015). Relative to other predatory species, the coyote has a significant impact on the livestock industry annually, however, its activity is severely exaggerated, leading to disproportionate efforts of eradication, or culling[1, 9, 21, 58] which have led a worsening conflict and even the spread of the species across the continent[46, 42, 53].

A common sentiment of managers and livestock owners when discussing coyote management and/or control is the phenomena of coyotes' ability to circumvent these efforts, due to their "cunning" intelligence. Thus, this species is acknowledged as unusually intelligent and cognitively and behaviorally adaptive, yet these capabilities have only been studied and quantified by only a few researchers, and just within the last six years[12, 75, 76, 77]. Yet, many have studied the spatial and movement ecology of *C. latrans*[5, 30, 31, 39, 53, 62, 77, 123].

Four searches were conducted using the American Public University System Richard G. Trefry Library, using four major databases (and additional specified databases within those major titles). Over all databases, search terms were "Canidae AND cognition AND dog" in Search 1, "Canidae AND cognition AND behavior" in Search 2-3, and one additional search was conducted using "*Canis* AND behavior AND cognition," as it was suspected that specifying the genus instead of the family would yield different results (Table 3.1).

Search #	Search Term(s)	Database(s)	Limits	Publication Date	Source Type	Document Type	Result Page Options	Yield
1	canidae AND cognition AND dog	ProQuest SciTech Collection (specifically: Agricultural Science Database, Biological Science Database, Environmental Science Database, Science Database)	Full Text, Peer-Reviewed	All dates	Scholarly Journals	Article, Case Study, Literature Review	Exclude duplicate documents	53
2	canidae AND cognition AND behavior	Elsevier Science Direct (in journals a. Animal Behavior and b. Applied Animal Behavior Science)	N/A	All dates: 2010-2019 (both time frames yielded same results)	N/A	Research Articles, Case Reports, Data Articles	N/A	2 1
3	canidae AND cognition AND behavior	EBSCOhost Academic Search Premier (specifically Academic Search Premier, Applied Science and Technology Source)	Find all my search terms; Apply related words; PDF Full Text; Scholarly (Peer-reviewed) Journals; [Special Limiters] Academic Journal, Article	N/A	N/A	Article	N/A	3
4	Canis AND behavior AND cognition	ProQuest SciTech Collection (specifically: Agricultural Science Database, Biological Science Database, Environmental Science Database, Science Database)	Full Text, Peer-Reviewed	All dates	Scholarly Journals	Article, Case Study, Literature Review	Exclude duplicate documents	515

Table 3.1. *Search parameters and results.*

Cognitive research in Canidae has almost exclusively focused on *C. l. familiaris* and *C. lupus*. This is interesting, as these are the two most closely related extant sister species within the *Canis* genus. There is disagreement on whether or not *C. latrans* is older than these two species (all of them having emerged within the last 5-2 mya[2, 61]) however, it is curious that comparative cognitive ethological research has not yet been applied to such a closely related Canid species which shares the same historical range and anthropogenic selection pressures as these two.

Research has found many distinct differences between wolves and dogs regarding their cognitive skill, mostly by use of the "loose string paradigm," a test which requires cooperation between conspecifics or heterospecifics (in the form of a human experimenter) to obtain food given two different conditions: delayed condition and dual tray condition. In the delayed condition, the animal must either wait for the con-/heterospecific partner, or *vice versa*, and simultaneously pull the ropes attached to a tray to bring food closer and receive the reward. In the dual tray condition, the requirements are the same, but the animal must realize that s/he must progress to the next tray with the partner, requiring an exercise of spatiotemporal cognitive skill as well. In all of these tests, wolves significantly outperformed dogs[67, 50]. Whether the dog dyads were composed of human-dog, two inexperienced dogs (had not solved the puzzles before) or mixed-experience dogs (one had solved the puzzles before while the other had not), their performance always fell short of the wolves' success rates in identical dyads. Dogs overall displayed more dependence on humans to solve the problem and demonstrated only slightly comparable cognitive skill to inexperienced wolf dyads [67, 50].

Dogs' reliance on humans to problem-solve as compared to wolves was highlighted even more where the two species were tested on persistence in attempting to solve an unsolvable task in the absence of humans[68].

Conspecific: of the same species

Heterospecific: of a different species

Here, wolves displayed greater persistence, almost a complete lack of neophobia toward the novel objects, a wider variety of motor diversity (different types of manipulation of the novel object, using teeth, snout, paw, etc.), a stronger ability to generalize (learning with object #1 that the task was unsolvable and so manipulated object #2 less) and more variation in behavioral syndromes between individuals[68]. Fugazza *et al.* (2018) found that *C. l. familiaris* puppies were more successful in learning problem-solving skills via oblique transmission (information transfer from an older, non-kin individual), as "scrounging" from mother may reduce the emergence of social learning.

A study which tested the three-dimensional spatial awareness of dogs *versus* wolves discovered that dogs do in fact display neotenous characteristics of ancestral canids, not only physically and behaviorally, but cognitively: dogs' performance in a test which required either random or ordinal pulling of both horizontal and vertical ropes was only slightly comparable to that of juvenile wolves[38].

Studies that focus specifically on the cognitive ethology of *C. latrans* are few and far between. So far, what is known of coyote cognition is that between natural habitats, rural and urban environments, coyote boldness and exploratory behavior significantly varies, with urban coyotes being the boldest (likely to engage in risky behavior) and exploratory (willing to explore/interact with novel environments and objects) of the three[12].

Regarding direct responses of coyotes to human activity, the extreme plasticity and adaptive capabilities of *C. latrans* has just begun to be demonstrated. Schultz & Young (2018) found that coyotes change their behaviors and space-use patterns in direct response to human activity: they become more vigilant and use perimeters, or edges, of habitats in the presence of humans, and, in the absence of humans, spend less than half of their time resting and use open spaces more frequently. This is in line with the known spatial ecology of the species[5, 39, 62]. Remarkably, *C. latrans* has also been found to be highly adaptive physiologically, having a rapid adrenocorticotropic hormone (ACTH) peak, where lag time in fecal glucocorticoid output (measured by fecal glucocorticoid monitoring, or FGM) was only eight hours, where congenerics such as African wild dogs, gray wolves and maned wolves were all approximately 24, 16-20 and 20, respectively. This means that coyotes face a significantly reduced fitness cost in the activation of the hypothalamic-pituitary-adrenal axis, as this negative feedback loop depletes available glucose over a long period of time, decreasing overall health and fecundity (Figure 3.1)[75].

Congenerics: of the same genus (wolves are in the taxonomic group *Canis* along with coyotes, etc.)

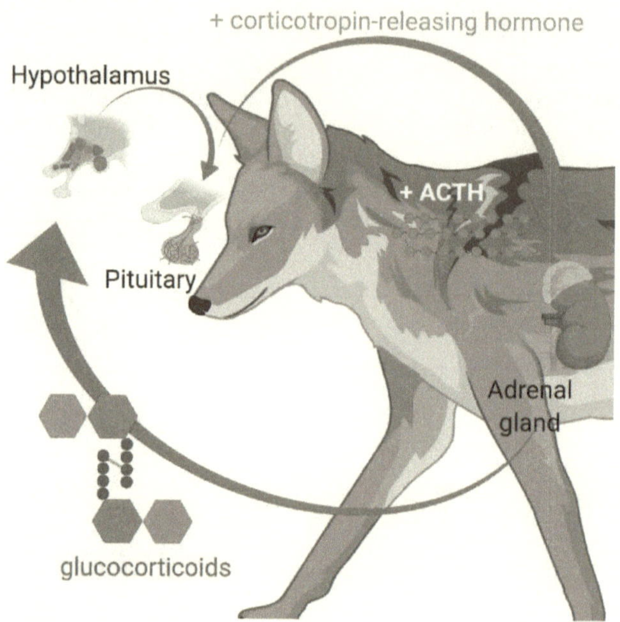

Figure 3.1. *Hypothalamic-pituitary-adrenal axis. This is a stress-induced physiological feedback loop, wherein the corticotropin-releasing hormone is released by the hypothalamus, stimulating the anterior pituitary gland. This results in the production of adrenocorticotropic hormone (ACTH). ACTH then stimulates the adrenal cortex to release glucocorticoids which then circulate back to the hypothalamus to end the negative feedback loop. Short-term activation of this feedback loop is highly adaptive because glucocorticoid production mobilizes stores of energy via increased gluconeogenesis; suppresses secondary physiological functions and enhances memory retention. However, in the long run, overproduction of glucocorticoids depletes glucose availability, resulting in physiological issues, thereby decreasing overall health and fecundity. Consequentially, chronic stress can be a significant threat to the fitness of an organism[75].*

These studies have significant implications for the management of *C. latrans*. From what we know of comparative cognitive studies on wolves and dogs, the ecological and behavioral plasticity of *C. latrans* may pose challenges to nonlethal management efforts, specifically hazing. The remarkable level of cognitive skill, spatial awareness and relative assertiveness (tendency to lead instead of follow, occurrences of stealing the rope from human partner in "loose string paradigm" tests)[67] demonstrated by wolves in all of these studies, demonstrate that coyotes may have a difficult time yielding solidified behavioral patterns (use of human resources, urban areas in their home ranges or roads as corridors) to behavioral modification efforts in the form of activities such as hazing. It seems that predictability of human behavior was helpful to the animals tested in the loose string paradigm, which means that nonlethal management efforts will need to be consistent between management authorities and civilian communities, a factor which has contributed to the failure of nonlethal management efforts in the past. Questions that arise from this knowledge are: Can coyotes accept information from humans in the form of hazing? Does habituation equate to a form of being "highly socialized?" (A trait which allowed dogs and wolves to cooperate well with humans, despite differences in cognitive ability.)

Additionally, the plasticity of coyote feeding ecology (hunter, scavenger, dependence on human resources) may impact persistence in novel tasks, making some coyotes more or less challenging with which to achieve behavioral modification. The species' behavioral, life history and socio-ecological plasticity may also influence cognitive skill — coyotes may ultimately fall anywhere between wolves and dogs in this regard.

My research aims to answer these questions. Nonlethal management is needed in the U.S., as federal efforts in predator control have disproportionately relied on lethal measures. This has accomplished nothing but exacerbating the problem of human-coyote conflict and threatens the balance of ecosystems all over North America. By developing an understanding of this "cunning" canid, nonlethal management efforts can be tailored to the cognitive skill and behavioral ecology of this animal, producing stronger, safer, more cost-effective and long-lasting results than management practices in the past.

Chapter 4. Ethical Exception

The dominant social paradigm of Western culture holds technological innovation, energy dominance, and expansion of civilization as its highest values. The cost, at this day in age, and as it has always been, is the health of the natural environment. Authorities, unfortunately, see the environment in terms of economic value – what services it can and cannot provide which further human prosperity. Ecological/environmental philosophers, or "ecosophers"[97], ecologists, conservationists and more, have been debating for centuries on how to communicate to the general public the degree to which humanity is dependent on the natural world. Humans do not exist apart from the earth, but are a part of an interdependent system, one living biota[21].

One set of ethics which attempts to change human behavior for the sake of preventing further environmental degradation is known as "deep ecology." Deep ecology is not an ethical school of thought which seeks to function within the confines of the existing dominant social paradigm. This ideology intends to completely reverse the modern way of thinking, specifically Western thinking, and encourage spiritual, metaphysical connection to the earth and its natural systems[23, 48].

Devall (1980) defines deep ecology as being based on Spinoza's biospheric egalitarianism, where all natural things are of equal value. One of the ways in which this ideology manifests is in the concept of "Unity" (one biota) instead of "dualism," (human and natural world), which is at the core of the dominant social paradigm[23].

The strength of the deep ecology ethic lies in the aspects which are known to science, and which are already at play in the world of research and philosophy. As Luke (2002) notes, some of deep ecology's foundational ideas are already exercised in modern society: "deep ecology has been developed by outdoorspersons – mountain climbers, backpackers, field biologists – with experience in observing natural phenomena and comes from the conservation/preservation movement." To extend legal rights and protection and moral considerability to all natural objects is a concern in the minds of ecologists, biologists, climatologists, nature enthusiasts and philosophers alike, whether they believe in a metaphysical connection to the earth or not. McCauley (2006) is an example of this, where it is argued that nature should not be valued based on ecosystem services, but on its own intrinsic value, apart from humankind. In a similar way of thinking, Rolston (2001) believes that natural objects do not need a human valuer for intrinsic value to exist within them. He says

Does it not rather seem that when we are describing what benefits the dragonflies or the snails, the plants with their leaf stomata, or the bacteria with their clocks, such value is pretty much fact of the matter. If we refuse to recognize such values as objectively there, have we committed some fallacy?

Great scientists such as Edward O. Wilson, in his book, *Letters to a Young Scientists*, highlight the fourth core idea of deep ecology which Devall (1980) outlines as the need for the "popular" scientific method to be done away with, and for the new focus of scientific research to be "objective" instead, specifically, "science should be both objective and participatory without modern science's subject/object dualism." Wilson expresses his passion for studying ants, not for the sake of pursuing any innovations for the sake of man, but for the sake of knowing the ant. In fact, this is why organizations such as The Wildlife Society (TWS), World Wildlife Fund (WWF), Convention on International Trade in Endangered Species of Wild Fauna and Flora (CITES) and International Union for Conservation of Nature (IUCN) exist. These organizations do not prioritize species conservation and research based on their economic value, but objectively, as Devall (1980) emphasizes. The animals are chosen and protected for their own sake, and for the sake of the biota in its entirety. These organizations exist, and function, as they do for one of the core, values Devall (1980) stresses: "Diversity is inherently desirable both culturally and as a principle of health and stability of ecosystems." It is a known scientific fact, whether ecologically or genetically, that biodiversity is a vital component to the persistence of populations of any flora or fauna. Without it, species are likely to bottleneck, and ultimately face the possibility of extinction.

One of the reasons why coyotes do not receive the same ethical consideration that many other species do is because wildlife managers and many consumptive users of public natural resources view the species as a threat to economic stability and capital gain. The coyote is purely competition for game species or a threat to livestock. There is no in-between or room for consideration of the species as an animal functioning naturally in its native environment. When an animal, or any being for that matter, is reduced to no more than a nuisance, there is no obligation to treat said animal as anything more. The moral responsibility to respect or value life is absent where no such life exists. The coyote becomes a caricature: a playing card of lobbyists fighting not for wildlife and environmental justice, but for the unfettered reign of the natural world.

A glaring weakness of deep ecology lies primarily in what Devall (1980) calls "reinhabitation:" "whereby men undertake activities and evolving social behavior that will enrich the life of the place, restore its life-supporting systems, and establish an ecologically and socially sustainable pattern of existence within it." Devall goes even further, quoting a 1979 Greenpeace editorial piece, to suggest that ultimately, following this ideology, that those who do not comply with activities which support a sustainable, healthy environment, will face "force," or physical punishment for such insubordination.

The reason this is a weakness is because of what deep ecology attempts to do, which is completely reverse the dominant social paradigm of Western society, and nearly, the world, by pushing the notion that humanity should essentially go back in time and return to a hunter-gatherer, politically decentralized societal structure, where subsistence is based on the land alone and progress is no longer defined by technological innovation but spiritual growth and connection to

Earth. Part of the issue with this is the assumption that everyone would ultimately fall into a "spiritual" belief system. Culturally, atheism is a characteristic of primarily Western culture. To ask this alone – for a society to essentially let go of scientific knowledge to pursue a metaphysical relationship over the quest for hard data – is a monumental task that would be met with much resistance.

Reinhabitation, which Luke (2002) indirectly describes as "anti-modern and future primitive," is part of the hypocritical nature of biocentrism that Watson (1983) discusses. To place restrictions on what humanity is allowed to do goes against the very foundation of biocentrism, which holds that man is no different from all other natural beings. To restrict man is to believe that man is separate, that man is different and "too powerful"[97]. Watson explains that it is simply a "nature's way," that man "[does] alter things." To believe anything different is a denial of man's ecological and evolutionary role, which again, contradicts biocentric egalitarianism – which deep ecology is based on – which says that all natural beings should be allowed to live to the full evolutionary potential.

What we are seeing now is a desperate imitation of reinhabitation. Many of those who practice a "Back to Basics" lifestyle are very much overlapping with people who still very much desire the separation of man and nature. The very ones who can for the death of a native, wild animal as soon as it does something our human fragility cannot take.

The danger in this is that we slowly inch our way toward the fantasy of human-controlled ecosystems every day. We push for the removal of apex predators and then claim that humans are responsible for Keeping prey species populations in check. It goes without saying that, regardless of our numbers, humans are simply incapable of taking up the role of more than one apex species, and any attempt to do so is informed by shameful arrogance. American communities must begin to recognize the importance of these animals alive and functioning in their native ecosystems.

Chapter 5. Time for Change

For years, California Fish and Game Code (CA FGC) Division 4 Chapter 3 Article 1 Sections 4150-4155 and with California Code of Regulations (CCR) Title (T) 14 Section 472, have allowed nongame mammals, that is, a mammal which is native to the state of California, which does not qualify as "game," is not protected federally or by the state, or not a fur-bearing mammal ["Fur-bearing mammals," according to CA FGC Div. 4 Ch. 2 Art. 1 §4000, includes "pine-marten, fisher, mink, river otter, gray fox, red fox, kit fox, raccoon, beaver, badger, and muskrat." "Game" includes both "small game" (CCR T14 §257) and "big game" (CCR T14 §350)] to be hunted without limit and at any time of year given only a handful of exceptions. These nongame species are the English sparrow, starling, domestic pigeon, coyote, weasels, skunks, opossums, moles and rodents (CCR T14 §472(a)). The coyote, *C. latrans*, is of particular concern here because, in this lineup, the coyote is the leading species in depredation-related livestock losses in the United States of America[56, 76], rising amounts of "wildlife damage"[14] nationwide, and are known carriers of disease such as Lyme disease and rabies[16]. The preferred method of control has been lethal control, and, in California, the statutes in question, CA FGC Div. 4 Ch. 2 Art. 1 §4000 and CCR T14 §472-475, in conjunction with – despite being native to North America – the coyote's perceived disposition as a nuisance, and in some cases, an ecologically functional invasive, species due its bolstering numbers nationwide, encourages the continuation of reliance on lethal efforts to eradicate *C. latrans*. Although lethal control certainly has a place in the management of *C. latrans*, there is more we can do to incorporate nonlethal management alternatives as it has been repeatedly proven that nonlethal control is not only more cost-effective but ecologically and agriculturally safer, with results having more long-term benefits[11, 27, 5]. Additionally, there are many ways in which exclusively lethal management can result in a variety of rebound effects[46, 42], leaving the coyote problem worse than it began.

All this considered, I argue that it is time to reform the California Fish and Game Code and Mammal Hunting Regulations, specifically regarding nongame mammals, to limit bag limits[4], and define limits to coyote open season (CA FGC Div. 0.5 Ch. 1 §62) based on credible science (CA FGC Div. 0.5 Ch. 1 §33) of the coyote's population ecology and biological life cycle. California hunting laws need to reflect current scientific knowledge and public values of all[90], and no longer lean in favor of specific socioeconomic or interest groups, namely hunters and farmers/ranchers[1,9].

CCR T14 §472-475 allows the legal possession of the previously listed nongame mammals and sets minimal restriction on "hours for taking:" overnight between dusk and dawn being the only prohibited times, in very specific locations closed to night hunting, which the policy goes on to define. The law is not applicable to the take of these nongame mammals with traps. The regulations proceed to set a handful more restrictions on the take of nongame mammals, including the prohibition of the use of poison, restriction of recorded bird or mammal calls to use only for the take of coyotes, bobcats, American crows and starlings, the prohibition of the simultaneous use of bait and hunting dogs, and the use of traps that are up to code and nonlead ammunition (CA FGC Div. 4 Ch. 3 Art. 1 §4150-4155, Art. 2 §4180-4190; CCR T14 §472-475).

This law has been used for the justification of staggering numbers of coyotes killed annually, nationwide, by federal agencies such as the USDA Wildlife Services (WS) and avid hunters participating in "hunting derbies," competitions in which hunters are rewarded with various prizes based on the amount of a given animal killed. These things have been done behind the defense of the idea that coyotes need to be controlled lethally due to the damage they impose on agriculture nationwide, and the practice of culling is a quick, direct (and "free," in some cases) and effective method of control. This is in opposition of scientific research which has proven nonlethal control to not only be more cost-effective, but to be generally the better management alternative, given that results are much longer-lasting and focus not only on the animal, but on human behavior as well[11, 27, 53].

The beginning of state authority over fish and wildlife is said to have begun in 1896 with the case of *Geer v. Connecticut*. In this case, Edward M. Geer was convicted of illegally taking, possessing and transporting woodcock, grouse, and quail beyond the boundaries of the state of Connecticut, 161 U.S. 519 (1896). This case was a defining moment that shaped the law that exists today, giving states the authority over fish and wildlife within their borders.

The California Fish and Game Commission first began in 1870 as the Board of Fish Commissioners, primarily concerned with fish in California waters. In 1909, the scope expanded to both fish and game, which merited a name change to what is now the Fish and Game Commission. Structural and political development led up to 1945, the year in which the California Fish and Game Commission (CFGC) officially assumed the responsibility and authority over-fishing and hunting regulation. CFGC maintains this responsibility, not only in distributing hunting and fishing licenses but determining appropriate times and limits on taking of specific species within the state.

Up until 2011, competitions referred to as "coyote hunting derbies," where hunters compete by killing the most, or biggest, coyotes for a variety of prizes including money and hunting gear, were entirely legal in California. These contests are not unique to the state, with pythons and feral hogs being the focus of competitions in states like Florida and Texas, respectively, California was the first in the nation to pass such a law. In a 4-1 vote, California Fish and Game Commission determined that the awarding of prizes for the killing of nongame species is "unethical and inconsistent" with current scientific knowledge and public values[24, 90]. The law went into effect in January of 2016:

*Except as specified in subdivisions (b), (c),
and (d), it is unlawful to offer a prize
or other inducement as a reward for the
taking of a game bird, mammal, fish, reptile
or amphibian in an individual contest,
tournament, or derby.... This section does
not apply to a person conducting an
individual contest, tournament, or derby for
the taking of a game bird or mammal, if the
total value of all prizes or other inducement
is less than five hundred dollars ($500) for
the individual contest, tournament, or
derby. (CA FGC Div. 3 Ch. 1
Sec. 2003 Subdiv. (a), (d))*

Advocates for coyote hunting defended the competitions by saying the hunters are a "population control or balance control for the predators"[71] and claims that those against the competitions are ignorant of the damage coyotes can cause. Part of what made these contests entirely legal was the fact that there is no limit on the number of coyotes that can be taken by an individual hunter at any given time of year. It was not required that life stage, season, location, the effect on sympatric species including predator release, or any other factor were considered in the lethal removal of a coyote by an individual hunter. Even now, this is still the case – the only change is that an individual may not legally take a coyote for profit or reward[4, 71].

This political attitude toward coyotes is not unique to California, or the individual hunter. According to Adkins (2018), USDA WS was responsible for killing 69,041 adult coyotes, plus an unknown amount of coyote pups killed by the destruction of 393 dens in 2017. This has massive implications due to two things: the rebound effect that HSUS (2017) defines as an increase in coyote numbers due to excessive reliance on lethal control can occur when there is a 50%-70% reduction in coyote populations[11, 42]; USDA WS methods result in stunning numbers of non-target species being killed in efforts to eradicate animals such as coyotes. Between 1990-2011, USDA WS killed 1,516 federally endangered gray wolves, 3,295 Western Great Lakes gray wolves, 9 Mexican gray wolves and hundreds of thousands more federally endangered, threatened and petitioned species[9]. To support an unlimited take policy on a species private and federal groups aim to eradicate nationwide is dangerous, even if one exclusively considered the massive nontarget species that are killed in this practice.

Wolves are mentioned in particular, because this is a species that can easily be mistaken for a coyote. In fact, this was one concern that played a role in the creation of the ban on coyote hunting derbies[4]. Additionally, research has shown increased rates of hybridization between coyotes and wolves[9, 44, 72], making the continuation of the unlimited take regulation much more dangerous. In the case of USDA WS, nontarget fatalities are excused under the "incidental take permit" defined in the Endangered Species Act (ESA) Section 10:

> *The Secretary may permit, under such terms*
> *and conditions as he shall prescribe… any*
> *taking otherwise prohibited by section*
> *9(a)(1)(B) if such taking is incidental to,*
> *and not the purpose of, the carrying out of*
> *an otherwise lawful activity.*

However, this is not applicable to individuals, although it has been used as an excuse for the take of endangered wolves by individual hunters in the past. One very well-known example is *United States of America vs. Chad Kirch McKittrick*, where McKittrick, among many other allegations, claimed that, when charged with the illegal take, possession, and transport of a federally endangered gray wolf, he was not aware that he was shooting a gray wolf but some other species, 142 F.3d 1170 (9th Cir. 1998). With increased rates of hybridization between wolves and coyotes, as officials in California Fish and Game Commission considered, this circumstance will progress to no longer be an excuse for illegal behavior, but a genuine possibility as coyotes attain more wolf-like attributes such as larger body sizes[44, 72].

As previously noted, HSUS (2017) asserts that one possible rebound effect of lethal management of coyotes could lead to an increase of coyote numbers due to sudden rise of reproduction rates as a consequence of the disruption of family groups and an increase in the number of breeding females. HSUS (2017) and Breck *et al.* (2017) note that this happens only when losses reach 50%-70% of the total population. When considering the nationwide popularity of coyote hunting derbies and the large numbers of losses due to USDA WS annually, it is entirely possible that, nationwide, at least 50% of the American coyote population has been lethally removed over time, which explains the ever-growing numbers of coyotes in urban areas throughout the country. This is all despite the National Wildlife Research Center's (NWRC), the research department of USDA WS, focus, which is to develop "socially acceptable and economically feasible methods for reducing wildlife damage impacts on agriculture, human health and safety and threatened and endangered species, while minimizing risks for humans, wildlife and the environment"[14]. Bergstrom *et al.* (2014) commented on this contradiction between official intents and actions by recalling that the American Society of Mammalogists "repeatedly from 1924 to 2012 criticized federal wildlife control programs as overly reliant on lethal measures, driven by special interests rather than science..."

According to USDA (2011), California, New Mexico, Oklahoma and Texas were states which lost the most cattle and calves to predators in the nation in 2010, at 9,600, 9,900, 13,900, and 46,000, respectively. In the entire country, 220,000 (5.5%) cattle and calves of the total 3.99 million lost that year, were lost to predators. Coyotes were determined to be responsible for 116,700 (53.1%) of the heads lost to predators, representing $48,185 nationwide. In California, coyotes accounted for 57% of cattle losses, 25.9% in New Mexico, 35.7% in Oklahoma, and 22.2% in Texas. For calves, coyotes were responsible for 75.7% losses in California, 65.2% in New Mexico, 52.6% in Oklahoma, and 40.1% in Texas. In New Mexico and Texas, coyotes came in second to mountain lions and bobcats for cattle losses[76].

There is no denying that coyotes have a significant impact on agricultural loss in the United States. However, when looking at the numbers, one must note that approximately 2.25% of all losses (predator and nonpredator), $48,185 nationwide does not merit the highly disproportionate efforts to eradicate this species by private and federal parties. This point takes on even more significance when considering that the main defense for culling coyotes is that it is the most effective, direct form of management. McManus *et al.* (2015) showed that, by transitioning to nonlethal management, farmers in the Eastern Cape Province of South Africa saved a mean of $20,000 (equivalent to the value of 138 livestock) in the first year. Additionally, these farmers experienced significant decreases in livestock depredation by 51-68%[53]. To base the practice of this regulation of no limit on take and time of taking, and the justification of USDA WS on the idea that lethal hunting is somehow a more efficient method of control is completely invalid. Breck *et al.* (2017) and Elliot *et al.* (2016) both note that part of what will help create effective coyote management policy is the management of humans as well. This entails a change in behavior of "risky" behaviors, which encourage and/or allow coyotes to increase levels of habituation, making human-coyote conflict more likely[11, 27].

Andrés *et al.* (2012) defines five different types of rebound effects that can occur due to "ineffective biodiversity policy:" biodiversity rebound I ("spatial spillover"), biodiversity rebound II (inconsistency in results of policy on different types of biodiversity), ecological rebound, service rebound, and environmental rebound. I argue that the "biodiversity" being protected is domestic, agricultural biodiversity and that the effects are biodiversity rebound II, ecological rebound and environmental rebound[46].

Andrés *et al.* (2012) define biodiversity II as a policy that prioritizes one type of biodiversity (genetic) over another (taxonomic or functional), resulting in negative effects on the latter. Research has shown that this is occurring, again, in the hybridization of coyotes and wolves[10, 44, 72]. Bohling *et al.* (2016) found 96 coyotes and nine hybrids living alongside 75 red wolves in the Red Wolf Experimental Population Area in North Carolina. Kays *et al.* (2010) discovered a "genetic swarm" in Northeastern USA where coyote and eastern wolf hybrids were also confirmed with genetic sampling, while Rutledge *et al.* (2011) found behavioral changes in both wolves and coyotes result in interspecies mating choices in Algonquin Provincial Park in Ontario, Canada. As those hunters who participate in coyote hunting derbies – which, despite them being banned, does not mean an end to limitless hunting on coyotes in the state of California – and USDA WS continue to value the health of agricultural stock over virtually anything else, these effects will begin to show in western states. These management methods and unbounded hunting regulations have resulted in taxonomic, and therefore functional changes of both coyotes and wolves in the eastern United States[10, 44]. Kays *et al.* (2010) noted that the larger body size and altered cranial morphology has led coyotes to even change their diets, as they are more capable of taking down larger prey like deer, unlike their counterparts in the West.

Secondly, ecological rebound is similar to part of biodiversity II, as this rebound results in biodiversity changes which lead to a variety of "responses in ecosystem functioning" (Andrés *et al.*, 2012). These responses can be either expected or unexpected, stemming from behavioral changes which result in coyotes and wolves interbreeding, and urban ecological changes in the abundance, behavior and feeding habits of competing urban species such as raccoons, feral cats, and skunks (32; Gehrt & Prange, 2006; Prange & 30). As coyotes are lethally removed from populations, this acts as a predator release on the previously listed species, resulting in an increase in nuisance behavior from them, also potentially resulting in an increased spread in specific diseases. With the intense pressure on coyotes nationwide, in combination with removal of wolves, the nearing of the 50% minimum removal of the species will inevitably result in the rebound reproductive surge HSUS (2017) discusses, ultimately creating dramatic changes in ecosystem functioning of a great number of species that either compete with, or are preyed upon by, the coyote.

Lastly, these two rebounds come together in what Andrés *et al.* (2012) call "environmental rebound." This is when ineffective biodiversity policy results in the creation of another environmental problem. For decades, coyotes have been increasing in levels of habituation, and for years, they have been growing in numbers while hunters and USDA WS vehemently claim that lethal control works. The country has seen that it doesn't. Culling is still a method officials depend on to control coyotes nationwide, accounting for 28.9% of all control methods. In California, it accounts for 5.2% of management practices, 9.2% in New Mexico, 24.7% in Oklahoma, and 31.4% in Texas. Management officials and scientists around the country are seeing the environmental rebound effect every year. California Mammal Hunting Regulations Chapter 6 §473-475 is not working, but contributing to new problems in the environment.

Regulations in California which allow coyotes, as nongame mammals "to be taken at any time of year and in any number..." has contributed to a growing problem in the country that shows in the practices of individual/groups of hunters, and federal agencies such as USDA Wildlife Services. The intense focus on coyotes is disproportionate to their economic impact on the country as a whole, as they only account for about 2.25%, that is, less than $50,000 in cattle and calf losses, for example, per year[76]. Yet, the USDA WS killed nearly 70,000 adult coyotes and an additional unknown number from the almost 400 dens destroyed. All of this is still separate from an unknown amount killed in coyote hunting derbies in states other than California – which are still quite popular and entirely legal throughout the country, as California was the first to pass such a law[4, 71].

Thankfully, in 2011, officials of the California Fish and Game Commission recognized that events that celebrated this regulation such as coyote hunting derbies were not in line with current scientific knowledge or public values[4, 71]. Still, what needs to come next is an explicit limit on the number of coyotes that can be taken during a hunting event, and a specified coyote hunting season which reflects current scientific knowledge of the coyote life cycle.

These changes are necessary because, with the disproportionate focus on coyotes as a pest species throughout the nation, a variety of rebound effects can result, not only increasing coyote numbers but contributing to – and even creating – entirely new environmental problems[46, 42]. I argue that the rebound effects which are already in progression include a sharp increase in reproduction rates due to massive disturbance of the coyote population[42], biodiversity II, ecological and environmental rebound effects[46]. Bohling *et al.* (2016), Kays *et al.* (2010) and Rutledge *et al.* (2011) have all demonstrated the majority of these phenomena to be in effect, as coyotes have been proven to be hybridizing with eastern coyotes in the eastern United States and Canada. California must implement a policy change before we begin to see such effects in western states.

It is no longer acceptable to defend such laws on the amount of "wildlife damage"[14] that coyotes have inflicted, or the supposed efficiency of lethal control. When considering all the numbers, coyotes account for only a small fraction of livestock losses annually[76] and lethal control of the species has been shown to be the least effective, more expensive alternative between that and nonlethal management[11, 27, 53]. It is time that California law reflects these facts.

I propose that, in combination with this policy change, there be a statewide no-feeding ordinance that addresses the feeding of feral cats. This is to reduce the number of attractant behaviors that bring coyotes to urban and suburban neighborhoods[27]. Feral cats themselves, apart from the food, are also attractants to coyotes as a prey item[32, 42].

Management officials need to also consider the role that human behavior plays in the growing problem of human-coyote conflict. According to Elliot *et al.* (2016), people regularly engage in risky, attractant behaviors including leaving food and/or small pets outside, and some demonstrate a poor understanding of what is appropriate and inappropriate behavior in the even that one would meet a coyote in person (8% of respondents said they would act in a way that results in the coyote snarling, growling, following or physically attacking the respondent or their pet)[27]. When policy begins to reflect an understanding of human responsibility in human-wildlife conflict, there will be a significantly decreased need for, and justification of, lethal removal of nuisance species, and thereby the elimination of justifications which support such policies as California Mammal Hunting Regulations Chapter 6 §473-475.

Example Management and Coexistence Plan

An Experimental Approach to Developing an Adaptive Management Plan

Proposals for Institutional Change

I propose that there be transformative, legislative change for USDA APHIS WS, and that these changes reflect public values, and all stakeholders, private interests and individual citizens regarding both consumptive and non-consumptive uses of natural resources, including wildlife. Additionally, these changes reflect the most up-to-date research provided by WS's own research department, USDA APHIS National Wildlife Research Center (NWRC)[11, 52, 76, 77].

I propose an amendment to the 1931 ADC Act (7 U.S.C. §426), which suspends the allowance of funding to WS by private stakeholders, thereby eliminating any potential conflicts of interest which jeopardize the protection of, and respect toward, natural resources, including *all* native wildlife.

I propose that there be definitive change in WS's terms of "wildlife damage," and that terms and circumstances of damage be given more clarity and specific boundaries, so that cases such as that of Greenwood Village, CO, where people are able to request the lethal removal of a coyote for its neutral presence in a given neighborhood, are no longer able to happen.

On the state level, I propose reform to CCR T14 §472-475 and CA FGC Div 4 Ch 3 Articles 1 and 2 in that CA FGC Div 1 Ch. 2 Article 1 §203.1 is applied to *all* animals including *C. latrans* in reference to methods of take allowed; "Credible science," as defined by CA FGC Div 0.5 Ch 1 §33, is applied to the determination of restrictions applied to the take of *C. latrans*, including consideration of plasticity in behaviors, seasons of life history (mating, pup-rearing and dispersal seasons – thereby eliminating perpetual "open season"), area of take (natural vs. rural landscapes) as this is a direct influence on the type of subpopulation and lastly, social structure of coyotes (transient vs. resident pack), where alpha residents should be excluded from take, as they are likely the sole reproductive pair in the home range and their removal would lead to immigration and further reproduction by transients[46, 42, 53].

There be a definitive bag and possession limit as defined by CA FGC Div 0.5 Ch 1 §18-19, 86.

I propose that federal, state and local governments put forth greater effort in public education and outreach, and efforts to implement *pro*active nonlethal methods are increased and standardized.

Further, it should be acknowledged the current political climate that exists around wildlife management is largely driven by the need to satiate special interest communities, namely hunters and agricultural professionals. This is not without justification, as revenue earned from recreational and substantive hunting plays a significant role in wildlife management and maintenance and protection of natural resources. However, let it be stated that this is not the only source of funding, and consumptive users of wildlife and natural resources are not the only ones who contribute to, and benefit from, these resources. That being said, all stakeholders, contributors, etc. should be considered and consulted in the development and implementation of wildlife and natural resources management.

With regard to agricultural professionals, of course, there should be an immense amount of respect paid to this community, as they feed the citizens of America, whether they are a part of large corporate farms or a local community shared agriculture (CSA). From wildlife managers and scientists, there should be a certain sensitivity applied when discussing the fate of such farmers and ranchers, because, although losses attributed to coyotes on a national scale pale in comparison to non-depredation-related causes, to lose one or more livestock can be a devastating blow to the individual farmer. All of this considered, it must be reiterated that these are not the only constituents affected by disproportionate lethal control to a native apex predator. Bergstrom *et al.* (2013) noted that over 70 million Americans spend $55 billion and produce more than $100 billion in total on *nonconsumptive* uses of wildlife and natural resources, "especially on federal public lands"[9]. The consumer base for nonconsumptive uses of wildlife and natural resources is vast, so it makes little sense that the values of this constituency are neglected, relative to those whose uses are primarily consumptive.

To begin seriously and consistently implementing nonlethal management practices would not be to the detriment to any of these parties, but to the benefit of all. Especially that it has been shown by McManus *et al.* (2014) that not only is nonlethal management more effective, but also more economically efficient: In the first year of implementing nonlethal control, the average total cost-per-head of management decreased by 59% over 11 farms. In this same year, depredation declined by 73.9%, and an additional 13.3% in the following nonlethal year. At the end of the study, McManus *et al.* reported that "[a]ll farms had a positive profit:loss ratio compared to lethal control, saving a mean of USD 5.36 for every USD 1 spent"[53].

Transformative change to legislation, public perception and behavior, and the manifestation of values of wildlife and natural resources through reprioritization and reconciliation of relational values between American citizens and federal, state and local governments need to take place in order for wildlife managers to start anew in the way *C. latrans* is treated. This change must begin by understanding, appreciating and applying the most recent, reputable, relevant research on *C. latrans* and its complex behavioral, movement and cognitive ecology, separating the American public from the myths of the historical war on coyotes.

Executive Summary

This management plan focuses on *Canis latrans*, the coyote, which has spread rapidly throughout the United States and is now being considered an invasive species[96]. Instead of shrinking populations due to encroachment, which is the fate of most species in developing regions, their numbers are growing, and the coyote population continues to grow throughout North America.

Despite *C. latrans* contribution to livestock losses in the United States being profoundly exaggerated, this species is the leading cause of depredation according to the USDA[58, 84]. In 2010, *C. latrans*, depredation accounted for 5.2% of a total 4.3% loss of cattle and calves. *C. latrans* was responsible for 53.1% of this, representing $48, 185. In 2015, *C. latrans* accounted for 40.5% of cattle depredation losses and 53.1% of calf losses, in the same year, depredation amounted to 5.2% of losses in the industry[58, 84]. Although this does not address losses of other livestock such as sheep and goats, this illustrates the relatively low level of general coyote impact on livestock and agricultural nationwide, yet tremendously high when compared to other predators (in descending order: mountain lions, bobcats, dogs, vultures, wolves, bears, other predators, unknown)[58].

As Beaumont, Banning and Cherry Valley, CA are rural cities, rapidly developing and growing in the context of the metropolitan Riverside County, the potential for human-coyote conflict grows, and proactive, adaptive management to prevent further conflict is needed.

This plan proposes two distinct components to proposed management actions: human management and coyote management. The human management side focuses on the reduction of coyote attractant behaviors such as leaving food outside and leaving small pets unattended, education on how and why to cease these behaviors, and a standardized process for record-keeping. The coyote

management aspect centers on combatting coyote habituation within and around the management area.

Monitoring activities will be conducted year-round, community surveys taking place in the middle of breeding, pup-rearing and dispersal seasons and public education efforts being emphasized in pup-rearing and dispersal seasons. Camera trapping will be used to estimate population sizes and monitor behavioral patterns, particularly habituation stages of local coyotes.

This plan is deemed to be necessary indefinitely. Data analysis and reassessment of management actions will be conducted at the end of every calendar year, to determine management actions for the following year.

Coexistence is included in the intent of this plan, as it is not an option to completely exclude coyotes from the human environment. As humans spread and urbanize more natural land, encroachment forces local fauna to either adapt to human presence or be eradicated. The coyote has been tremendously successful at the former, and so it is our duty to ensure that both urban wildlife and humans maintain a healthy, safe environment, even with this forced sympatry.

Introduction

Canis latrans, the coyote, was once restricted to the southwest and plains regions of the United States, Canada, and Mexico. Since colonization, the species has spread north and west, with the removal of wolves contributing to their expansion throughout North and Central America[34].

In recent years, as human encroachment on natural habitat increases, coyote populations throughout the country have adapted to human activity with continuously rising levels of habituation[7] and the species has become increasingly bold and, consequentially, problematic[11]. This is of great concern, as the coyote is a known sentinel species for diseases including Lyme disease, rabies, plague and tularemia[16, 21, 79] and is capable of spreading diseases such as mange and distemper to domestic dogs[79, 122]. Although their impact is often exaggerated it is true, that *C. latrans* has been responsible for the losses of millions of dollars in livestock animals over the past several decades[96] and believed to have an increasingly harmful role on populations of deer, caribou, rabbit, sea turtle and more species, in their respective regions[96]. Although, from a more positive perspective, they have been observed to mitigate the negative impacts imposed by feral cat populations on local bird, rodent and rabbit species[13].

Reports of incidents and sightings of coyotes have skyrocketed in recent years[7,66] to the point that the Humane Society of the United States published a Template Coyote Management and Coexistence Plan in 2017. Cities that have employed their own adaptations of the template plan include Inglewood, Calabasas, Huntington Beach, Costa Mesa and more. Beaumont, Banning, and Cherry Valley, CA are not included in this list. Coyote abundance has been found to be positively correlated with human presence and activity and has been observed to prefer urban edges[62], roads/corridors[5, 41], agricultural land and grassland[5, 39]. Yet, this species is highly adaptive and has also been known to coniferous woodland, mountains, chaparral, and desert habitats.

The cities of Beaumont, Banning and Cherry Valley, CA are rapidly growing cities consisting largely of agricultural landscapes. These cities are located within an area in southern California categorized as "suburban" in California's bioregions. Although there have been fewer reports of coyote sightings and interactions submitted in recent years in this area, as opposed to other counties within Southern California[66], the potential for coyote population growth and resulting human-coyote conflict is rising.

One major source of division on the reduction of human-coyote conflict is whether or not culling[1, 9, 21, 58] is the most efficient solution to the economic, environmental and social losses due to the species. In a number of areas, hunters are

encouraged and paid and/or rewarded for shooting and killing coyotes. In California, according to the California Fish and Game Commission, coyotes are one of the non-game species that can be hunted "at any time of year and in any number," with some regulations on time of day and method of the hunt (CAFGC, 2018). Part of HSUS's goal is to inform the public that exclusively lethal management does not work and only leads to a "rebound effect," where significant losses in coyote populations lead to increased reproduction[46, 42, 53].

This plan aims to manage both humans[27] and coyotes. Management actions will incorporate nonlethal proactive and lethal proactive and reactive management[11] according to the Baker & Timm (1998) scale of habituation, alongside public education efforts focused on the reduction of coyote attractant behaviors[7, 27] and standardized record-keeping of incidents and sightings[7, 66].

Vision Statement

The vision of this Coyote Management & Coexistence Plan is to reduce human-coyote conflict in a collaborative effort to secure the health and safety of the people and animals of Beaumont, Banning and Cherry Valley, CA, with the use of public education and continuous ecological research.

Stakeholder Groups

Some of the stakeholder groups that will be invited to collaborate in the implementation of this management plan, and the reasoning for their inclusion, include:

Riverside County Environmental Health: The reasoning for the inclusion of this stakeholder is that coyotes are categorized under Carnivores of Public Health Significance by the California Department of Public Health (CDPH)[16]. These carnivores are considered a threat to public health because they pose a threat of physical trauma via bites or other means of physical conflict with humans, and transmission of infectious diseases to humans and domestic animals[16, 21, 79]. Reducing the occurrence of coyotes within and around city boundaries can significantly reduce the risk of transmission of diseases such as rabies, plague, tularemia, mange, and distemper.

California Department of Fish and Wildlife: The reasoning for the inclusion of this stakeholder is that this department manages one of the wildlife areas surrounding Beaumont, Banning and Cherry Valley: San Jacinto Wildlife Area. This is listed as a study area as a means of monitoring space and resource utilization of coyotes in surrounding natural areas, in order to monitor changes in species behavior when comparing anthropogenic vs. natural resource use as a result of management actions.

United States Department of Agriculture Forest Service: The reasoning for the inclusion of this stakeholder is that this department manages one of the wildlife areas surrounding Beaumont, Banning and Cherry Valley: San Bernardino National Forest. The use of this study area is that which is listed for the stakeholder directly above.

California Department of Parks and Recreation: The reasoning for the inclusion of this stakeholder is that this department manages one of the wildlife areas surrounding Beaumont, Banning and Cherry Valley: the San Jacinto Mountains. The use of this study area is that which is listed for the stakeholder directly above.

Municipalities (residents and leadership) of Beaumont, Banning, and Cherry Valley, CA: Beaumont, Banning and Cherry Valley are all relatively small neighboring cities in Riverside County. The United States Census Bureau estimated the population of Beaumont to be at 46.967, a 27.6% growth since 2010 and Banning at 31,230, a 5.5% since 2010. Cherry Valley population estimates are not available for 2017, however, in 2010, it was estimated to be home to 6,362 people. The area in total is undergoing urbanization at a rapid rate, and with no coyote management plan in place, with its agricultural and growing city landscape, the potential for human-coyote conflict is becoming a primary concern.

ívïluwenetem Metémak (Cahuilla) People: Beaumont, Banning, and Cherry Valley lie in the ancestral lands of this Indigenous community. They are the rightful custodians of this land and all that inhabit it. Their relationship with the coyote stretches back for millennia, presenting an invaluable wealth of cultural knowledge integral to interspecies coexistence, though those not belonging to this community are not entitled to such knowledge. Still, any hope of an effective, equitable coyote management plan beholden to their leadership.

Goals and Associated Objectives

There are two primary goals, and their associated objectives, of this management plan:

> 1. To reduce human behaviors and activities that encourage coyote presence and habituation.

a. Reduce attractants in the form of human behaviors (i.e. engaging coyotes in direct contact, leaving small pets unattended in yards) and food availability (i.e. feeding feral cats)[7, 27]. Attractant behaviors that residents of Beaumont, Banning and Cherry Valley will be determined by a survey of communities primarily along urban edges, near agricultural landscapes[39, 62], and near forested areas (near wildlife areas/parks), which coyotes use as corridors[5].

b. Record keeping for sightings and incidents will be standardized between the three cities to ensure accurate communication and shared information[7, 66].

c. Lastly, education of communities in the aforementioned habitat types on coyote behavior and avoidance techniques, especially during pup-rearing and dispersal seasons will be implemented to further reduce coyote attractant behaviors[39, 66].

2. To counteract and prevent further habituation of local coyote populations.

a. Nonlethal proactive management for coyotes displaying habituation stages 1-2[7].

b. Lethal proactive management for coyotes displaying habituation stages 3-4[7].

c. Lethal reactive management for coyotes displaying habituation stages 5-7[7].

Resource Overview
Focal Species

C. latrans were believed to have been restricted to the south-west and plains regions of the United States, Canada, and Mexico prior to European settlement. The species is native to Belize, Canada, Guatemala, Honduras, Mexico, Nicaragua, Panama, and the United States[34].

C. latrans is a highly adaptive predator, as an omnivorous, opportunistic predator that is flexible in many different environments, preferring open areas such as prairies and desert[42]. When in urban environments, the coyote has been observed to be most partial to shrubs and other woody vegetation, agricultural landscapes, grassland, and urban edges[5, 39, 62]. The coyote is a monogamous species, and further, only the alpha pair of coyotes in any given pack reproduce, with the subordinate individuals helping care for pups. The average litter size averages between 4-7 pups and gestation lasts 62-65 days. Mating season is January-April, followed by pup-rearing season from May-August and finally dispersal season September-December[66].

As mentioned above, the coyote primarily feeds on rodents, fruit, deer and rabbit, although they are opportunistic and maintain omnivorous diets, especially in urban environments [Gerht, 2007; 42]. They are known to feed on deer as carrion.

As an adult, a coyote can weigh between 25-35 pounds, and, height- and length-wise is similar in size to a German Shepherd Dog. They can live in packs consisting of 5-6 individuals, including the breeding pair. These packs do not hunt together, however, they do depend on the entire unit to defend their established territory. The species can live in two distinct lifestyles, "resident" and "transient." Resident coyotes are those that live in a group setting, and, as defined by Hinton *et al.* (2015), are "individuals (breeders, juveniles, and pups) belonging to a pack and in possession of a territory that exhibit passive (i.e., scent-marking) and aggressive (i.e., physical conflict) behaviors to exclude conspecifics[39]." Transient coyotes are nomadic, often having a loosely defined home range, but no distinct territorial boundaries. These transient coyotes are a critically important source of understanding the species behavior in terms of space use and their general ecology, naturally, and in

urban settings [30, 39]. Transients are also important in that they tend to be the ones which develop behavioral tendencies that lead them to become "problem individuals"[11].

The cities included in this management plan are Beaumont, Banning and Cherry Valley (unincorporated), California.

These cities are located in southwestern California, in the northwestern portion of Riverside County. Beaumont and Cherry Valley are primarily rural, with resident families owning livestock species of cattle, horses, sheep, goats, and chickens, typically. All three cities have been categorized in the Western Riverside County Multiple Species Habitat Conservation Plan to be included in the San Bernardino Mountains Bioregion. The plan defines this area as consisting of coniferous forests, montane chaparral, and broad-leaved forest. The cities are located in a region categorized as "urban."

The area of Beaumont, CA is 31.4 mi^2; the city of Banning directly west is 22.8 mi^2 and Cherry Valley, an unincorporated community just north of Beaumont is approximately 8.2 mi^2.

Management Alternatives

There are two management alternatives aside from the chosen coexistence management plan. The two plans exclusively focus on human and coyote management, respectively.

Goal: Alter human behavior within Beaumont, Banning and Cherry Valley, CA to reduce coyote-attractants, and therefore, coyote presence, within the management area.

Objectives:

1. Survey communities of Beaumont, Banning and Cherry Valley, CA, primarily along urban edges and near agricultural landscapes, grassland, and natural corridors[5, 39, 62].

2. Public education efforts on how to reduce attractant behaviors based on the results of surveys.

This management alternative focuses on the investigation of coyote-attractant behaviors that residents of Beaumont, CA may engage in, and proceeds to educate the public on cessation of these behaviors based on findings. Elliot *et al.* (2016) argue that "managing *people* is crucial to coexistence." This study found that people will more often than not, fail to "make the connection" between human behavior, coyote behavior, and resulting conflict[27].

Management cannot rely too heavily on community-level hazing as a dominant component of management/control, as the public tends to be inconsistent in its application of the practice, and hazing is not yet scientifically proven to be effective[11]. Elliot *et al.* (2016) found that people

who had a more positive perspective of coyotes (lower fear scores and higher "Nature Attitude" scores) were less likely to haze, as compared to those who displayed opposite scores of high fear scores. Additionally, those that "believed that urban coyotes were a nuisance" were more likely to haze. Elliot *et al.* (2016) also found that "residents with more positive views of urban wildlife had riskier behaviors that attract coyotes." All of this suggests that, among senior and homeless/lower-income demographics of the relevant cities (D. Dodge, California Department of Fish and Wildlife, pers. comm., 2018), animal lovers, at least those individuals with a relatively positive attitude toward coyotes, need to be a target group in education efforts in reducing coyote-attractant behaviors in the context of human management.

Both Quinn *et al.* (2016) and Hinton *et al.* (2015) have found that peak quantity in coyote sighting and incident reports are submitted in pup-rearing season (May-August) and dispersal season (September-December). Increased education efforts should be employed during these times, especially to those demographics previously specified.

Coyote Management

Goal: Counteract habituation of present coyote populations and prevent habituation of present and new coyote populations.

Objectives:

1. Proactive and Reactive Control Methods:

a. Nonlethal proactive management will be used on coyotes displaying habituation stages 1-3. Nonlethal proactive management is defined by Breck *et al.* (2017) as: "Altering the behavior of coyotes prior to the onset of conflict." This typically involves hazing or "aversive conditioning"[11].

b. Lethal proactive management will be used on coyotes displaying habituation stages 4. Lethal proactive management is defined by Breck *et al.* (2017) as: "Removal of urban coyotes prior to the onset of severe conflict." Breck *et al.* (2017) suggest that this control method be used year-round and based on behavioral patterns of individuals selected for removal.

c. Lethal reactive management will be used on coyotes displaying habituation stages 5-7. Lethal reactive management is defined by Breck *et al.* (2017) as: "Removal of urban coyotes after severe conflict occurs. Removal efforts are focused at the location of conflict with the goal of removing the individual or individuals causing conflict."

Progression of Habituation in *Canis latrans* as described by Baker & Timm, 2017	
Level 1	More frequent presence of coyotes in human-dominated areas such as streets and yards, especially at night.
Level 2	Increase in frequency of occurrences in which coyotes take domestic pets and/or *non-aggressively* approach humans.
Level 3	Coyotes present in human-dominated areas such as streets, recreational parks, and yards throughout the day.
Level 4	Coyotes taking or chasing domestic pets in the
Level 5	Coyotes attacking and taking pets that are on-leash and/or in close proximity to owners. Coyotes may also pursue people jogging, biking, or pedestrians.
Level 6	Coyotes present in/near children's areas: schools, play areas, parks, in the daytime.
Level 7	Coyotes acting aggressively toward adults in the daytime.

Table 1. *Baker & Timm (2017) defines a scale of habituation displayed by coyotes in urban environments. This table will be used to determine what management action needs to be taken for the control of individual coyotes based on behavior.*

This plan will define "severe conflict" as Baker & Timm (2017) define "attacks:" "when physical contact between 1 or more non-rabid coyote(s) and 1 or more person(s) [or pet(s)/livestock] occurred at a single location at a point in time, when contact was not initiated by the person(s) [or pet(s)/livestock]."

There is much more research that needs to be done on transiency and the development of problem individuals[11], and so far, it has been observed that transient individuals are a key component to the ecology of coyotes as a species [30, 39]. Removing individuals who display inappropriate levels of habituation, and/or are the cause of severe conflict can reduce the chances of negative incidents in the future.

Monitoring Activities

This plan will undergo constant monitoring in the form of community surveys, incident and sighting reports and camera trapping along urban edges and corridors. Each management stage will last one calendar year. Data will be analyzed at the end of each stage to determine success and future management actions. For the first stage, there will need to be a period of six months before the first calendar year of the management plan to collect preliminary data to use as a baseline.

As coyotes are living creatures that evolve over time through adaptation to a constantly changing environment, and the cities of Beaumont, Banning and Cherry Valley, California are continuously growing, this plan, at this moment in time, is determined to be necessary indefinitely.

Community Surveillance

Residents will be asked to report coyote sightings and incidents using Coyote Cacher (Figure 2; Dr. Niamh Quinn, University of California Cooperative Extension, Orange County, 2017) to keep the process of recording sightings and incidences simple and streamlined.

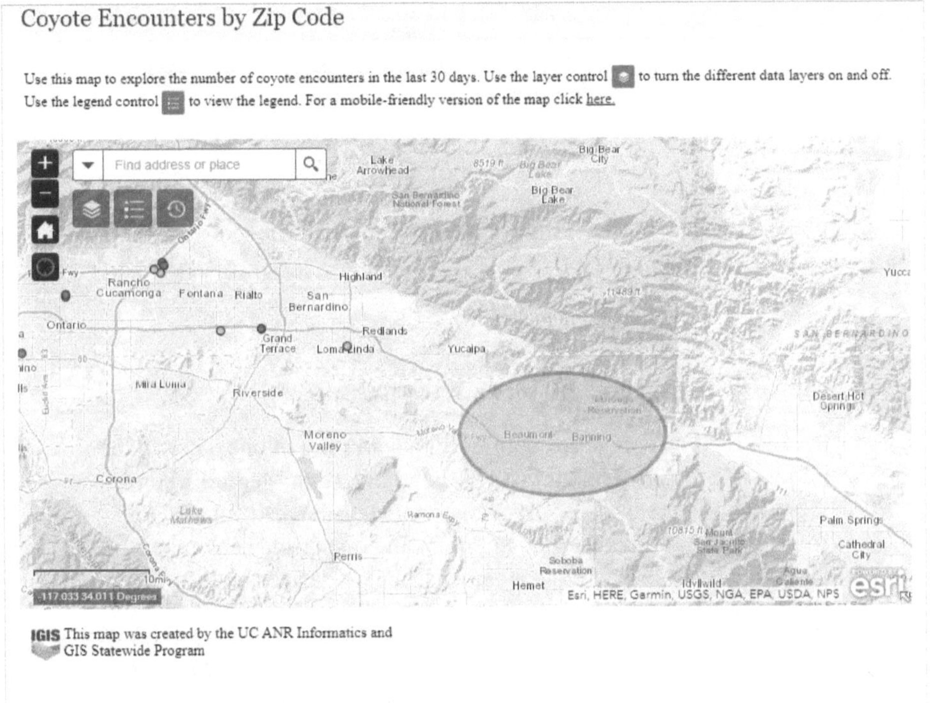

Figure 1. Coyote Cacher interactive map. The value of this program relies on making relevant communities aware of it as a resource for coyote reports. Residents can submit reports following a category list organized in the following levels: Green, Level 1: Sighting only, Pet missing; Yellow, Level 2: Coyote advanced towards or appeared to follow reports, Chased pet off-leash – no contact between coyote and pet, Pet attacked off leash – contact between coyote and pet; Red, Level 3: Chased pet on-leash – no contact between coyote and pet, Pet attacked on-leash – contact between coyote and pet, Pet killed by coyote, Coyote bit reporter. (UC ANR Informatics and GIS Statewide Program, 2018)

Coyote Surveillance

Camera trapping will be used along urban edges, corridors, agricultural landscapes and grasslands to estimate coyote population size and monitor behavioral patterns within the study area[5, 11, 39, 62].

Assessment and Success Criteria
Analysis of Community Surveillance

Analysis of data collected from community surveys will be evaluated with Chi-square test,

$$x^2 = \Sigma_n \frac{(O-E_i)^2}{E_i}, \; df\,N\text{-}1, \; \mathrm{p} < 0.05 \; \textbf{(1)}$$

to determine possible relationships between survey responses. A two-tailed binomial test

$$R_{Crit} = \left(\frac{(N-1)}{2}\right) - k\sqrt{(n+1)}\mathrm{k} = 0.9880 \; \textbf{(2)}$$

will be used to analyze the survey responses as well.

Surveys will be conducted online for the duration of one week in the middle of breeding (January-April; February 15 to March 15 being identified as "the middle"), pup-rearing (May-August; June 15 to July 15 being defined as "the middle") and dispersal (September-December; October 15 to November 15 being defined a "the middle") seasons.

Survey questions will measure attitude toward coyotes and human behavioral patterns toward coyotes partially following the questionnaire goals outlined in Elliot *et al.* (2016): to investigate residents' attitudes and fears regarding urban coyotes and other urban wildlife, personal experiences with coyotes, potential attractant behaviors residents may be engaging in and "socio-demographics information (age, sex, race/ethnicity, education, income, place of residence, number of children, number and type of pets)"[27].

Management actions, regarding the human aspect, will be determined successful when resident attitudes increase in positivity (fear responses lower, primarily), attractant behaviors lessen in frequency and spread (the number of neighborhoods in which residents engage in attractant behavior is reduced) and rate of pet/livestock loss is significantly reduced. Data will be analyzed by a t-test,

$$t = \frac{(\bar{x}_1 - \bar{x}_2)}{sqrt\left(\left(\frac{\sigma_1^2}{n_1}\right) + \left(\frac{\sigma_2^2}{n_2}\right)\right)}, \; df\,n1\text{-}n2\text{-}2 \; \textbf{(3)}$$

and significant change will be measured by a two-tailed binomial test (Equation 1).

The success of nonlethal proactive, and lethal proactive/reactive management will be determined by analysis methods used by Breck *et al.* (2017): Time elapsed between removal events will be measured to calculate recurrence. Recurrence will be defined as a removal event occurring more than once in a given area where two home ranges overlap, which will be calculated with the "overlap" package in R[11, 55].

Coyote population size will be estimated during winter and summer, as Breck *et al.* (2017) point out that, during these times, the population consists of adults, then adults and pups, respectively. Estimating the population size will allow for the calculation of the percentage of coyotes being removed due to conflict. Coyote abundance and species richness will be estimated with the Shannon-Weiner index[46, 69].

The estimated number of coyote packs will be multiplied by 15% to account for transient individuals[11].

A 95% confidence interval will be calculated for all values: "number of packs, pack size, number of residents and transients, and population size"[11].

Coyote movement ecology will be analyzed and quantified using space-use, movement and management alternative models[6, 21, 35, 65] and R packages, "lme4," "rptR," and "MCMCglmm" (Hertel *et al.*., 2019). Home ranges of both transients and residents will be determined using the ADK method[5, Worton, 1989].

A unique aspect of this study is that it will emphasize the role of animal cognition in the development of problem individuals and the effectiveness of nonlethal management methods. This is currently a knowledge gap in the field of behavioral and urban ecology in relation to coyotes[11]. To better understand the developmental process of "problem individuals"[11], behaviors of transient individuals and resident packs will be analyzed using non-parametric Mann-Whitney U test, and the "glmmADMB" and "lsmeans" packages in R[3, 77].

Management actions may be deemed successful when a significant reduction in the percentage of coyotes removed due to conflict, lowered rates of use of anthropogenic resources and significantly lower rates of recurrence in negative coyote incidents. Significance will be calculated using a t-test (Equation 3), with a value of significance set to $p < 0.05$ and the correlation of behavioral changes in relation to management methods will be tested with a chi-squared test (Equation 2).

Learning and Feedback/Adaptation

This is an adaptive management plan. Adaptive management focuses on a learning-based approach to managing natural resources. Moore (2009) defines adaptive management as

> *... a structured process of learning by doing.*
> *It is based on a flexible framework that*
> *allows managers to adapt their practices as*
> *the relationship between people and the*
> *environment changes.*

As previously mentioned, this management plan will be implemented in stages lasting one calendar year. A preliminary data collection period will be necessary before the first management stage to create a baseline to which data analyzed at the end of said management stage will be compared. Analysis of data from each following management stage will be compared to the preceding stage.

What this accomplishes is a constant feedback loop of learning and resulting action.

Before data collection begins, stakeholders will discuss what aspects of management will be of focus: community health in relation to the coyote being a sentinel species for rabies, plague, and tularemia[16, 21, 79]; local economies, considering livestock/agricultural losses by coyotes consuming livestock and fruits/vegetables; social welfare, in light of coyotes attacking/consuming pets, and attacking/scaring residents.

Reliant on data results from management stage two, there is potential to alter the plan so that lethal proactive management is no longer a key component of coyote control. This would further reduce the potential for creating a rebound effect.

Community participation in terms of reducing coyote attractant behaviors will also play a crucial in determining the need, or lack thereof, for lethal proactive management. This, again, will be decided based on data analysis following management stage two.

Jazmin (nickname: "Sunny") Murphy studied zoology at the University of California, Santa Barbara and graduated with a Bachelor's in 2015. She is now pursuing a Master of Science degree in Environmental Policy and Management with American Public University, with a focus on Fish and Wildlife Management. Her current and future work focuses on the intersection of canid ecology with Black and Indigenous histories in the United States. This entails multifaceted, cross-disciplinary examinations of conceptions of wildlife and "nature" within opposing dominant social paradigms, as informed by cultural histories and lifeways, and how that dominant social paradigm, along with economic and political paradigms, inform and direct the management of canid species, or predators in general.

You can follow Jazmin's work and reach out to collaborate at **blackflowercontentwriting.services**.

Bibliography

1. Adkins, C. (2018). Agricultural department killed 1.3 million native animals in 2017: Ignoring calls for reform, Wildlife Services slaughtered coyotes, bears, wolves. Retrieved from https://www.biologicaldiversity.org/news/press_relea ses/2018/wildlife-services-04-23-2018.php
2. Agnarsson, I., Kuntner, M., & May-Collado, L. J. (2010). Dogs, cats, and kin: A molecular species-level phylogeny of Carnivora. Molecular Phylogenetics and Evolution, 54(3), 726-745. doi:10.1016/j.ympev.2009.10.033
3. Agresti, A. (2013). Categorical data analysis. Hoboken, NJ: John Wiley & Sons.
4. Associated Press Staff. (2014, December 3). California's OK with hunters killing coyotes — but not for prizes. Retrieved from https://www.ocregister.com/2014/12/03/californias-ok-with-hunters-killing-coyotes-but-not-for-prizes/
5. Atwood, T. C., Weeks, H. P., & Gehring, T. M. (2004). Spatial ecology of coyotes along a suburban-to-rural gradient. Journal of Wildlife Management, 68(4), 1000-1009. doi:10.2193/0022-541x(2004)068[1000:seocaa]2.0.co;2
6. Baker, C. M. (2016). Target the source: Optimal spatiotemporal resource allocation for invasive species control. Conservation Letters, 10(1), 41-48. doi:10.1111/conl.12236
7. Baker, R. O., Timm, R. M. (2017). Coyote attacks on humans, 1970-2015: implications for reducing the risks. Human-Wildlife Interactions 11(2):120-132.
8. Barrett, L. P., Stanton, L. A., & Benson-Amram, S. (2019). The cognition of 'nuisance' species. Animal Behaviour, 147, 167-177. doi:10.1016/j.anbehav.2018.05.005
9. Bergstrom, B. J., Arias, L. C., Davidson, A. D., Ferguson, A. W., Randa, L. A., & Sheffield, S. R. (2013). License to

kill: Reforming federal wildlife control to restore biodiversity and ecosystem function. Conservation Letters, 7(2), 131-142. doi:10.1111/conl.12045

10. Bohling, J. H., Dellinger, J., McVey, J. M., Cobb, D. T., Moorman, C. E., & Waits, L. P. (2016). Describing a developing hybrid zone between red wolves and coyotes in eastern North Carolina, USA. Evolutionary Applications, 9(6), 791-804. doi:10.1111/eva.12388

11. Breck, S. W., Poessel, S. A., Bonnell, M. A. (2017) Evaluating lethal and nonlethal management options for urban coyotes. Human-Wildlife Interactions 11(2):133-145.

12. Breck, S. W., Poessel, S. A., Mahoney, P., & Young, J. K. (2019). The intrepid urban coyote: a comparison of bold and exploratory behavior in coyotes from urban and rural environments. Scientific Reports, 9(1). doi:10.1038/s41598-019-38543-5

13. Brown, B., Crosdale, T. & Melendez, N. 17 July 2015. Episode 4: Cats and Coyotes [Audio podcast]. Urban Wildlife Podcast. Retrieved from www.urbanwildlifecast.com/?p=71.

14. Bruggers, R. L., Owens, R., & Hoffman, T. (2002). Wildlife damage management research needs: perceptions of scientists, wildlife managers, and stakeholders of the USDA/Wildlife Services program. International Biodeterioration & Biodegradation, 49(2-3), 213-223. doi:10.1016/s0964-8305(02)00042-2

15. Bull, J. W., Ejrnaes, R., Macdonald, D. W., Svenning, J., & Sandom, C. J. (2018). Fences can support restoration in human-dominated ecosystems when rewilding with large predators. Restoration Ecology, 27(1), 198-209. doi:10.1111/rec.12830

16. California Department of Public Health. (2009). Vertebrates of Public Health Importance in California. Fritz, Curtis L. (Ed.). Sacramento, CA: California Department of Public Health.

17. California Fish and Game Commission. (2018). About the California Fish and Game Commission. Retrieved from http://www.fgc.ca.gov/public/information/

18. California Fish and Game Commission. (2018). Mammal Hunting Regulations 2018-2019. Retrieved from http://www.fgc.ca.gov/regulations/current/mammalregs.aspx#472.

19. California Fish and Game Commission. (2018). Mammal hunting regulations 2018-2019. Retrieved from http://www.fgc.ca.gov/regulations/current/mammalregs.aspx#472

20. Callicott, J. B. (1987). Chapter 9: The conceptual foundations of the land ethic. In Companion to a Sand County Almanac (pp. 186-217).

21. Chomel, B. B., Morton, J. A., Kasten, R. W., & Chang, C. (2016). Case Report: First Pediatric Case of Tularemia after a Coyote Bite. Case Reports in Infectious Diseases, Article ID 8095138. Retrieved from http://dx.doi.org/10.1155/2016/8095138.

22. Conner, M. M., Ebinger, M. R., & Knowlton, F. F. (2008). Evaluating coyote management strategies using a spatially explicit, individual-based, socially structured population model. Ecological Modelling, 219(1-2), 234-247. doi:10.1016/j.ecolmodel.2008.09.008

23. DeCandia, A. L., Henger, C. S., Krause, A., Gormezano, L. J., Weckel, M., Nagy, C., ... VonHoldt, B. M. (2019). Genetics of urban colonization: neutral and adaptive variation in coyotes (Canis latrans) inhabiting the New York metropolitan area. Journal of Urban Ecology, 5(1). doi:10.1093/jue/juz002

24. Devall, B. (1980). The deep ecology movement. Natural Resources Journal, 20(2), 299-322. Retrieved from http://digitalrepository.unm.edu/cgi/viewcontent.cgi?article=2860&context=nrj

25. Draheim, M. (2012). *Social conflict and human-coyote interactions in suburban Denver* [Doctoral

dissertation]. http://ebot.gmu.edu/bitstream/handle/1920/7860/Draheim_dissertation_2012.pdf?sequence=1&isAllowed=y

26. Ellington, E. H., & Gehrt, S. D. (2019). Behavioral responses by an apex predator to urbanization. Behavioral Ecology, 30(3), 821-829. doi:10.1093/beheco/arz019

27. Elliot, E. E., Vallance, S., & Molles, L. E. (2016). Coexisting with coyotes (Canis latrans) in an urban environment. Urban Ecosystems, 19(3), 1335-1350. doi:10.1007/s11252-016-0544-2

28. Fugazza, C., Moesta, A., Pogány, Á., & Miklósi, Á. (2018). Social learning from conspecifics and humans in dog puppies. Scientific Reports, 8(1). doi:10.1038/s41598-018-27654-0

29. Geer v. Connecticut

30. Gehrt, S. D. (2007). Ecology of coyotes in urban landscapes. In Proceedings of the 12th Wildlife Damage Management Conference (pp. 303-311). Dundee, IL: School of Environment and Natural Resources, Ohio State University and Max McGraw Wildlife Foundation.

31. Gehrt, S. D., Anchor, C., & White, L. A. (2009). Home range and landscape use of coyotes in a metropolitan landscape: Conflict or coexistence? Journal of Mammalogy, 90(5), 1045-1057. doi:10.1644/08-mamm-a-277.1

32. Gehrt, S. D., Wilson, E. C., Brown, J. L., & Anchor, C. (2013). Population ecology of free-roaming cats and interference competition by coyotes in urban parks. PLoS ONE, 8(9), e75718. doi:10.1371/journal.pone.0075718

33. Gerht, S. D. (2009). Home Range and Landscape Use of Coyotes in a Metropolitan Landscape: Conflict or Coexistence?. Journal of Mammalogy, 90(5): 1045-1057.

34. Gese, E.M., Bekoff, M., Andelt, W., Carbyn, L. & Knowlton, F. (2008). Canis latrans. The IUCN Red List of Threatened Species 2008: e.T3745A10056342.

Retrieved from
http://dx.doi.org/10.2305/IUCN.UK.2008.RLTS.T3745
A10056342.en.

35. Gum, R., Arthur, L. M., & Magleby, R. S. (1978). Coyote
control: A simulation of evaluation of alternative
strategies (408). USDA Economics, Statistics and
Cooperatives Service.

36. Hennessy, C. A., Dubach, J., & Gehrt, S. D. 2012. Long-
term pair bonding and genetic evidence for monogamy
among urban coyotes (Canis latrans). Journal of
Mammalogy 93(3), 732-742. doi:10.1644/11-MAMM-
A-184.1

37. Hertel, A. G., Leclerc, M., Warren, D., Pelletier, F.,
Zedrosser, A., & Mueller, T. (2019). Don't poke the
bear: Using tracking data to quantify behavioural
syndromes in elusive wildlife. Animal Behaviour, 147,
91-104. doi:10.1016/j.anbehav.2018.11.008

38. Hiestand, L. (2011). A comparison of problem-solving
and spatial orientation in the wolf (Canis lupus) and
dog (Canis familiaris). Behavior Genetics, 41(6), 840-
857. doi:10.1007/s10519-011-9455-4

39. Hinton, J. W., van Manen, F. T, Chamberlain, M. J.
(2015). Space Use and Habitat Selection by Resident
and Transient Coyotes (Canis latrans). PloS One 10(7):
e0132203. doi:10.1371/journal.pone.0132203.

40. Hody, J. W., & Kays, R. (2018). Mapping the expansion
of coyotes (Canis latrans) across North and Central
America. ZooKeys, 759, 81-97.
doi:10.3897/zookeys.759.15149

41. Holden, M. H., Nyrop, J. P., & Ellner, S. P. (2016). The
economic benefit of time-varying surveillance effort for
invasive species management. Journal of Applied
Ecology, 53(3), 712-721. doi:10.1111/1365-
2664.12617

42. Humane Society of The United States. (2017). A
template coyote management & coexistence plan.
Retrieved from

http://www.humanesociety.org/assets/pdfs/wildlife/template-coyote-management-plan.pdf

43. IUCN SSC Antelope Specialist Group 2016. Antilocapra americana (errata version published in 2017). The IUCN Red List of Threatened Species 2016: e.T1677A115056938. http://dx.doi.org/10.2305/IUCN.UK.2016-3.RLTS.T1677A50181848.en.

44. Kays, R., Curtis, A., & Kirchman, J. J. (2010). Rapid adaptive evolution of northeastern coyotes via hybridization with wolves. Biology Letters, 6(1), 89-93. doi:10.1098/rsbl.2009.0575

45. Keohane, M. N., & Olmstead, S. M. (2007). Markets and the environment (2nd ed.). Washington, DC: Island Press.

46. Linnell, J. D. C., Aanes, R., Swenson, J. E., Odden, J., & Smith, M. E. 1997. Translocation of carnivores as a method for managing problem animals: A review. Biodiversity and Conservation 6, 1245-1257

47. Lloyd, M., & Ghelardi, R. J. (1964). A Table for Calculating the `Equitability' Component of Species Diversity. The Journal of Animal Ecology, 33(2), 217. doi:10.2307/2628

48. Luke, T. W. (2002). Deep ecology: Living as if nature mattered. Organization & Environment, 15(2), 178-186. doi:10.1177/10826602015002005

49. Maestre Andrés, S., Calvet Mir, L., Van den Bergh, J. C., Ring, I., & Verburg, P. H. (2012). Ineffective biodiversity policy due to five rebound effects. Ecosystem Services, 1(1), 101-110. doi:10.1016/j.ecoser.2012.07.003

50. Marshall-Pescini, S., Basin, C., & Range, F. (2018). A task-experienced partner does not help dogs be as successful as wolves in a cooperative string-pulling task. Scientific Reports, 8(1). doi:10.1038/s41598-018-33771-7

51. Mason, E. 2006. Value Pluralism. The Stanford Encyclopedia of Philosophy. Retrieved from

https://plato.stanford.edu/archives/spr2018/entries/value-pluralism/.

52. McCauley, D. J. (2006). Selling out on nature. Nature, 443(7107), 27-28. doi:10.1038/443027a

53. McClennen, N., Wigglesworth, R. R., Anderson, S. H., & Wachob, D. G. (2001). The effect of suburban and agricultural development on the activity patterns of coyotes (Canis latrans). The American Midland Naturalist, 146(1), 27-36. doi:10.1674/0003-0031(2001)146[0027:teosaa]2.0.co;2

54. McManus, J. S., Dickman, A. J., Gaynor, D., Smuts, B. H., & Macdonald, D. W. (2014). Dead or alive? Comparing costs and benefits of lethal and non-lethal human–wildlife conflict mitigation on livestock farms. Oryx, 49(04), 687-695. doi:10.1017/s0030605313001610

55. Meredith, M., & Ridout, M. (2018). Overview of the overlap package. Retrieved from https://cran.r-project.org/web/packages/overlap/vignettes/overlap.pdf

56. Mitchell, B. R., Jaeger, M. M., & Barrett, R. H. (2004). Coyote depredation management: current methods and research needs. Wildlife Society Bulletin, 32(4), 1209-1218. doi:10.2193/0091-7648(2004)032[1209:cdmcma]2.0.co;2

57. Much, R. M., Breck, S. W., Lance, N. J., & Callahan, P. (2018). An ounce of prevention: Quantifying the effects of non-lethal tools on wolf behavior. Applied Animal Behaviour Science, 203, 73-80. doi:10.1016/j.applanim.2018.02.012

58. National Agricultural Statistics Service. (2000). Sheep and goat predator loss. Retrieved from United States Department of Agriculture website: https://downloads.usda.library.cornell.edu/usda-esmis/files/6108vb26w/gf06g540m/c821gn602/sgpl-05-05-2000.pdf

59. National Agricultural Statistics Service. (2011). Cattle death loss. Agricultural Statistics Board, United States Department of Agriculture.

60. Nitzschner, M., Melis, A. P., Kaminski, J., & Tomasello, M. (2012). Dogs (Canis familiaris) evaluate humans on the basis of direct experiences only. PLoS ONE, 7(10), e46880. doi:10.1371/journal.pone.0046880

61. Nyakatura, K., & Bininda-Emonds, O. R. (2012). Updating the evolutionary history of Carnivora (Mammalia): a new species-level supertree complete with divergence time estimates. BMC Biology, 10(1), 12. doi:10.1186/preaccept-53989005761110216

62. Ordenaña, M. A., Crooks, K. R., Boydston, E. E., Fisher, R. N., Lyren, L. M., Siudyla, S., Haas, C. D., Harris, S., Hathaway, S. A., Turschak, G. M., Miles, A. K., & van Vuren, D. H. (2010). Effects of Urbanization on carnivore species distribution and richness. Journal of Mammalogy, 91(6):1322-1331.

63. Palmer, C. (2012). An overview of environmental ethics. In L.P. Pojman & P. Pojman (Eds.) Environmental ethics: Readings in theory and application, 6th ed., 10-35.

64. Pienaar, E. F., Kreye, M. M., & Jacobs, C. (2015). Conflicts between cattlemen and the Florida panther: Insights and policy recommendations from interviews with Florida cattlemen. Human Ecology, 43(4), 577-588. doi:10.1007/s10745-015-9765-x

65. Quaglietta, L., & Porto, M. (2019). SiMRiv: an R package for mechanistic simulation of individual, spatially-explicit multistate movements in rivers, heterogeneous and homogeneous spaces incorporating landscape bias. Movement Ecology, 7(1). doi:10.1186/s40462-019-0154-8

66. Quinn, N., Fox, D. & Hartman, J. (2016) An examination of citizen-provided coyote reports: temporal and spatial patterns and their implications for management of human-coyote conflicts [Video File]. 30 Coyote Management & Coexistence

67. Range, F., Marshall-Pescini, S., Kratz, C., & Virányi, Z. (2019). Wolves lead and dogs follow, but they both cooperate with humans. Scientific Reports, 9(1). doi:10.1038/s41598-019-40468-y

68. Rao, A., Bernasconi, L., Lazzaroni, M., Marshall-Pescini, S., & Range, F. (2018). Differences in persistence between dogs and wolves in an unsolvable task in the absence of humans. doi:10.7287/peerj.preprints.26913v1

69. Roberts, N. J. (2011). Investigation into survey techniques of large mammals: surveyor competence and camera-trapping vs. transect-sampling. Bioscience Horizons: The International Journal of Student Research, 4(1), 40-49. doi:10.1093/biohorizons/hzr006

70. Rolston, H. (2001). Naturalizing values: Organisms and species. In L.P. Pojman (Ed.) Environmental ethics: Readings in theory and application, 3rd ed., 78-89.

71. Rott, N. (2014, December 4). California bans coyote killing contests. Retrieved from https://www.npr.org/2014/12/04/368408213/california-bans-coyote-killing-contests

72. Rutledge, L. Y., White, B. N., Row, J. R., & Patterson, B. R. (2011). Intense harvesting of eastern wolves facilitated hybridization with coyotes. Ecology and Evolution, 2(1), 19-33. doi:10.1002/ece3.61

73. Sanchez Rojas, G. and Gallina Tessaro, S. 2016. Odocoileus hemionus. The IUCN Red List of Threatened Species 2016: e.T42393A22162113. http://dx.doi.org/10.2305/IUCN.UK.2016-1.RLTS.T42393A22162113.en.

74. Sarkki, S., Ficko, A., Miller, D., Barlagne, C., Melnykovych, M., Jokinen, M., … Nijnik, M. (2019). Human values as catalysts and consequences of social innovations. Forest Policy and Economics, 104, 33-44. doi:10.1016/j.forpol.2019.03.006

75. Schell, C. J., Young, J. K., Lonsdorf, E. V., & Santymire, R. M. (2013). Anthropogenic and

    physiologically induced stress responses in captive coyotes. Journal of Mammalogy, 94(5), 1131-1140. doi:10.1644/13-mamm-a-001.1

76. Schell, C. J., Young, J. K., Lonsdorf, E. V., Santymire, R. M., & Mateo, J. M. (2018). Parental habituation to human disturbance over time reduces fear of humans in coyote offspring. Ecology and Evolution. doi:10.1002/ece3.4741

77. Schultz, J. T., & Young, J. K. (2018). Behavioral and spatial responses of captive coyotes to human activity. Applied Animal Behaviour Science, 205, 83-88. doi:10.1016/j.applanim.2018.05.021

78. Schwörer, T., Federer, R. N., & Ferren II, H. J. (2014). Invasive species management programs in Alaska: A survey of statewide expenditures, 2007–11. ARCTIC, 67(1), 20. doi:10.14430/arctic4359

79. Stone, J. T. (2016). A Serologic Survey of Coyotes (Canis latrans) for Canine Distemper in the Trans-Pecos Region of Texas [Master's Thesis]. Retrieved from https://search-proquest-com.ezproxy1.apus.edu/docview/1811954012?pq-origsite=summon.

80. The Humane Society of the United States. (2017). A template coyote management & coexistence plan. Retrieved from http://www.humanesociety.org

81. The United States Department of Agriculture: Animal and Plant Health Inspection Services. (2011). WS directive: Lethal control of animals (2.505). Retrieved from https://www.aphis.usda.gov/aphis/ourfocus/wildlifed amage/SA_WS_Program_Directives

82. U.S. Fish and Wildlife Service/Endangered Species Program. (2013, July 15). Endangered Species Program | Laws & Policies | Endangered Species Act | Section 10 Exceptions. Retrieved from https://www.fws.gov/endangered/laws-policies/section-10.html

83. United States Census Bureau. (2018). Quick Facts: Cherry Valley CDP, California; Beaumont city, California; Banning city, California. Retrieved from https://www.census.gov/quickfacts/fact/table/cherryv alleycdpcalifornia,banningcitycalifornia,beaumontcityca lifornia/PST045217.

84. United States Department of Agriculture, Animal and Plant Health Inspection Service, Veterinary Services, & National Animal Health Monitoring System. (2015). Sheep and lamb nonpredator death loss in the United States. Retrieved from United States Department of Agriculture website: https://www.aphis.usda.gov/animal_health/n ahms/sheep/downloads/sheepdeath/SheepDeathLoss 2015.pdf

85. United States Department of Agriculture, Animal and Plant Health Inspection Service, Veterinary Services, & National Animal Health Monitoring System. (2017). Death loss in U.S. cattle and calves due to predator and nonpredator causes, 2015. Retrieved from United States Department of Agriculture website: https://www.aphis.usda.gov/animal_health/nahms/ge neral/downloads/cattle_calves_deathloss_2015.pdf

86. United States Department of Agriculture, National Agriculture Statistics Service, & Agricultural Statistics Board. (2011). Cattle death loss. Retrieved from http://www.aphis.usda.gov

87. United States Department of Agriculture. (2017). Death loss in U.S. cattle and calves due to predator and nonpredator causes. USDA, Animal and Plant Health Inspection Service, Veterinary Services, National Animal Health Monitoring System.

88. United States Department of Agriculture. 2011. Cattle Death Loss.

89. United States Department of Agriculture: Animal and Plant Health Inspection Services. (2004). WS directive: The WS integrated wildlife management program (2.105). Retrieved from

https://www.aphis.usda.gov/aphis/ourfocus/wildlifed
amage/SA_WS_Program_Directives
90. United States Department of Agriculture: Animal and
Plant Health Inspection Services. (2009a). WS
directive: Mission and philosophy of the WS
program (1.201). Retrieved from
https://www.aphis.usda.gov/aphis/ourfocus/wildlifed
amage/SA_WS_Program_Directives
91. United States Department of Agriculture: Animal and
Plant Health Inspection Services. (2009b). WS
directive: Selecting wildlife damagement management
methods (2.101). Retrieved from
https://www.aphis.usda.gov/aphis/ourfocus/wildlifed
amage/SA_WS_Program_Directives
92. United States Department of Agriculture: Animal and
Plant Health Inspection Services. (2010). WS directive:
Code of ethics (1.301). Retrieved from
https://www.aphis.usda.gov/aphis/ourfocus/wildlifed
amage/SA_WS_Program_Directives
93. United States Department of Agriculture: Animal and
Plant Health Inspection Services. (2014). WS directive:
WS decision model (2.201). Retrieved from
https://www.aphis.usda.gov/aphis/ourfocus/wildlifed
amage/SA_WS_Program_Directives
94. United States of America v. Chad Kirch McKittrick
95. Van Eeden, L. M., Dickman, C. R., Ritchie, E. G., &
Newsome, T. M. (2017). Shifting public values and what
they mean for increasing democracy in wildlife
management decisions. Biodiversity and
Conservation, 26(11), 2759-2763.
doi:10.1007/s10531-017-1378-9
96. Ventosa-Febles, E. (31 January 2013). CABI: Invasive
Species Compendium: Canis latrans (Coyote):
Datasheet. Retrieved from
https://www.cabi.org/isc/datasheet/90296.
97. Watson, R. A. (1983). A critique of anti-anthropocentric
biocentrism. Environmental Ethics, 5(3), 245-256.
doi:10.5840/enviroethics19835325

98. Wildlife Services. (1996). Harvest and population data of selected reported species reported to the WS program, FY 1996. Retrieved from United States Department of Agriculture, Animal and Plant Health Inspection Services website: https://www.aphis.usda.gov/aphis/ourfocus/wildlifedamage/SA_Reports

99. Wildlife Services. (1997). Harvest and population data of selected reported species reported to the WS program, FY 1997. Retrieved from United States Department of Agriculture, Animal and Plant Health Inspection Services website: https://www.aphis.usda.gov/aphis/ourfocus/wildlifedamage/SA_Reports

100. Wildlife Services. (1998). Harvest and population data of selected reported species reported to the WS program, FY 1998. Retrieved from United States Department of Agriculture, Animal and Plant Health Inspection Services website: https://www.aphis.usda.gov/aphis/ourfocus/wildlifedamage/SA_Reports

101. Wildlife Services. (1999). Harvest and population data of selected reported species reported to the WS program, FY 1999. Retrieved from United States Department of Agriculture, Animal and Plant Health Inspection Services website: https://www.aphis.usda.gov/aphis/ourfocus/wildlifedamage/SA_Reports

102. Wildlife Services. (2000). Harvest and population data of selected reported species reported to the WS program, FY 2000. Retrieved from United States Department of Agriculture, Animal and Plant Health Inspection Services website: https://www.aphis.usda.gov/aphis/ourfocus/wildlifedamage/SA_Reports

103. Wildlife Services. (2001). Harvest and population data of selected reported species reported to the WS program, FY 2001. Retrieved from United

States Department of Agriculture, Animal and Plant Health Inspection Services website: https://www.aphis.usda.gov/aphis/ourfocus/wildlifed amage/SA_Reports

104.	Wildlife Services. (2002). Harvest and population data of selected reported species reported to the WS program, FY 2002. Retrieved from United States Department of Agriculture, Animal and Plant Health Inspection Services website: https://www.aphis.usda.gov/aphis/ourfocus/wildlifed amage/SA_Reports

105.	Wildlife Services. (2003). Harvest and population data of selected reported species reported to the WS program, FY 2003. Retrieved from United States Department of Agriculture, Animal and Plant Health Inspection Services website: https://www.aphis.usda.gov/aphis/ourfocus/wildlifed amage/SA_Reports

106.	Wildlife Services. (2004). Harvest and population data of selected reported species reported to the WS program, FY 2004. Retrieved from United States Department of Agriculture, Animal and Plant Health Inspection Services website: https://www.aphis.usda.gov/aphis/ourfocus/wildlifed amage/SA_Reports

107.	Wildlife Services. (2005). Number of animals killed and methods used by the WS program, FY 2005. Retrieved from United States Department of Agriculture, Animal and Plant Health Inspection Services website: https://www.aphis.usda.gov/aphis/ourfocus/wildlifed amage/SA_Reports

108.	Wildlife Services. (2006). Number of animals killed and methods used by the WS program, FY 2006. Retrieved from United States Department of Agriculture, Animal and Plant Health Inspection Services website:

https://www.aphis.usda.gov/aphis/ourfocus/wildlifed
amage/SA_Reports

109.   Wildlife Services. (2007). Number of animals
killed and methods used by the WS program, FY 2007.
Retrieved from United States Department of
Agriculture, Animal and Plant Health Inspection
Services website:
https://www.aphis.usda.gov/aphis/ourfocus/wildlifed
amage/SA_Reports

110.   Wildlife Services. (2008). Number of animals
killed and methods used by the WS program, FY 2008.
Retrieved from United States Department of
Agriculture, Animal and Plant Health Inspection
Services website:
https://www.aphis.usda.gov/aphis/ourfocus/wildlifed
amage/SA_Reports

111.   Wildlife Services. (2009). Table G. Animals
Taken by Wildlife Services - FY 2009. Retrieved from
United States Department of Agriculture Animal and
Plant Health Inspection Services website:
https://www.aphis.usda.gov/aphis/ourfocus/wildlifed
amage/sa_reports/sa_pdrs/sa_2009/ct_data_index_200
9

112.   Wildlife Services. (2010). Table G. Animals
Taken by Wildlife Services - FY 2010. Retrieved from
United States Department of Agriculture Animal and
Plant Health Inspection Services website:
https://www.aphis.usda.gov/aphis/ourfocus/wildlifed
amage/sa_reports/sa_pdrs/sa_2009/ct_data_index_201
0

113.   Wildlife Services. (2011). Table G. Animals
Taken by Wildlife Services - FY 2011. Retrieved from
United States Department of Agriculture Animal and
Plant Health Inspection Services website:
https://www.aphis.usda.gov/aphis/ourfocus/wildlifed
amage/sa_reports/sa_pdrs/sa_2009/ct_data_index_201
1

114.	Wildlife Services. (2011). Table G. Animals Taken by Wildlife Services - FY 2011. Retrieved from United States Department of Agriculture Animal and Plant Health Inspection Services website: https://www.aphis.usda.gov/aphis/ourfocus/wildlifed amage/sa_reports/sa_pdrs/sa_2009/ct_data_index_201 2

115.	Wildlife Services. (2011). Table G. Animals Taken by Wildlife Services - FY 2011. Retrieved from United States Department of Agriculture Animal and Plant Health Inspection Services website: https://www.aphis.usda.gov/aphis/ourfocus/wildlifed amage/sa_reports/sa_pdrs/sa_2009/ct_data_index_201 3

116.	Wildlife Services. (2014). Program Data Report G - 2014 Animals Dispersed / Killed or Euthanized / Removed or Destroyed / Freed or Relocated. Retrieved from United States Department of Agriculture Animal and Plant Health Inspection Services website: https://www.aphis.usda.gov/aphis/ourfocus/wildlifed amage/pdr/?file=PDR-G_Report?p=2014:INDEX:

117.	Wildlife Services. (2015). Program Data Report G - 2015 Animals Dispersed / Killed or Euthanized / Removed or Destroyed / Freed or Relocated. Retrieved from United States Department of Agriculture Animal and Plant Health Inspection Services website: https://www.aphis.usda.gov/aphis/ourfocus/wildlifed amage/pdr/?file=PDR-G_Report?p=2015:INDEX:

118.	Wildlife Services. (2016). Program Data Report G - 2016 Animals Dispersed / Killed or Euthanized / Removed or Destroyed / Freed or Relocated. Retrieved from United States Department of Agriculture Animal and Plant Health Inspection Services website: https://www.aphis.usda.gov/aphis/ourfocus/wildlifed amage/pdr/?file=PDR-G_Report?p=2016:INDEX:

119.	Wildlife Services. (2017). Program Data Report G - 2017 Animals Dispersed / Killed or Euthanized / Removed or Destroyed / Freed or Relocated. Retrieved from United States Department of Agriculture Animal and Plant Health Inspection Services website: https://www.aphis.usda.gov/aphis/ourfocus/wildlifed amage/pdr/?file=PDR-G_Report?p=2017:INDEX:

120.	Wildlife Services. (2018). Program Data Report G - 2018 Animals Dispersed / Killed or Euthanized / Removed or Destroyed / Freed or Relocated. Retrieved from United States Department of Agriculture Animal and Plant Health Inspection Services website: https://www.aphis.usda.gov/aphis/ourfocus/wildlifed amage/pdr/?file=PDR-G_Report?p=2018:INDEX:

121.	Williams, B.K., Szaro, R.C., & Shapiro, C.D. (2009). Chapter 3 How Should Adaptive Management be Implemented? (pp. 21-48). In Adaptive Management: The U.S. Department of the Interior Technical Guide. Adaptive Management Working Group, U.S. Department of the Interior, Washington, D.C.

122.	Wilson, E. V. (2012). The dynamics of sarcoptic mange in an urban coyote (Canis latrans) population (Master's thesis). Retrieved from https://urbancoyoteresearch.com/sites/default/files/r esources/Wilson_Evan_Thesis.pdf

123.	Young, J. K., Glasscock, S. N., & Shivik, J. A. (2008). Does spatial structure persist despite resource and population changes? Effects of experimental manipulations on coyotes. Journal of Mammalogy, 89(5), 1094-1104. doi:10.1644/07-mamm-a-198.1